Contents

D0506486

Introduction

Welcome to *Adobe Illustrator® 7.0 Classroom in a Book*,™ the most comprehensive guide available for learning how to use the Adobe Illustrator drawing program.

Prerequisites

Before beginning to use Adobe Illustrator, you should have a working knowledge of your operating system and its conventions, including how to use a mouse and standard menus and commands, and how to open, save, and close files. For help with any of these techniques, please see your Macintosh® or Microsoft® Windows® documentation.

About Classroom in a Book

Adobe Illustrator 7.0 Classroom in a Book is designed for beginning and intermediate users of Adobe Illustrator. If you're new to Adobe Illustrator, you'll learn all the important fundamental concepts and features you'll need to know to master the program in the first section of the book, Fundamentals. If you've been using Adobe Illustrator for a while, you'll find the second section of the book, *Beyond the Basics*, teaches many advanced features, including tips and techniques for using the latest version of Adobe Illustrator.

Each lesson and project concludes with a review section summarizing what you've covered. Taking time to read over the review sections will help you retain important concepts about the lesson and about Illustrator.

Free Web-based training from DigitalThink

Adobe Systems has partnered with DigitalThink, a leading Web-based training provider, to bring personalized instruction on Adobe Illustrator to your desktop. The online course *Illustrator Fundamentals* is included at no charge with your purchase of *Adobe Illustrator 7.0 Classroom in a Book*. An advanced course, *Mastering the Art*, is also available from DigitalThink.

 Look for the DigitalThink logo throughout this book for references to additional information in the online companion course.

About Illustrator Fundamentals

Designed for beginning Illustrator users, this online companion course expands on Illustrator techniques and functionality beyond what is covered in *Adobe Illustrator Classroom in a Book*. Here's a short list of course topics:

- Using the Illustrator grid
- Drawing complex geometric shape
- Rotating and twirling shapes
- Stroking outlines
- Drawing free-form paths
- Mixing corners and curves
- Hand-tracing in Illustrator
- Adding callouts to an illustration
- Creating a brief table using tabs
- Creating paths from character outlines

Expert instruction at your convenience

Both *Illustrator Fundamentals* and *Mastering the Art* are taught by Deke McClelland, a graphic design expert and best-selling author on Adobe products. In these courses McClelland shares his powerful tips and techniques for using Adobe Illustrator.

DigitalThink's Web-based training

At DigitalThink you can log on whenever you want, from wherever you have a Web connection. In both courses you can take dozens of new lessons, chart your progress with instantly scored and clearly explained quizzes, and polish your skills with hands-on exercises, all at your own pace. But you don't have to learn alone. All DigitalThink courses feature personal tutors, expert instructors, live chats, threaded discussions, and student-to-student conferencing. Live help is always just a mouse click away.

How to log in to your free DigitalThink course

To log in to the Web-based course included with *Adobe Illustrator Classroom in a Book*, you'll need to enter your unique access code. To locate your access code, turn to the back inside cover of this book, and remove the CD from the sealed envelope. Your 12-digit access code is printed on the back inside cover. Follow the instructions below to find out how to enter this code in DigitalThink's online registration form.

Important: The access code that comes with this book is valid for only one user. To purchase additional access codes to the introductory course, write to sales@digitalthink.com.

To register for the course:

1 Use a Web browser to go to http://www.digitalthink.com/partners/adobe/

2 The above URL takes you to a welcome page with instructions on how to register for either course. Read the instructions, then click the Register button next to *Illustrator Fundamentals* to enroll in your complimentary course. You will receive an on-screen registration form.

3 Fill in the on-screen registration form, and be sure to enter your unique discount code in the box labeled Discount Code.

How to purchase *Mastering the Art*

If you would like to purchase DigitalThink's intermediate- to advanced-level Illustrator course, point your browser to the URL above. When you see the welcome page, locate the Register button next to *Mastering the Art.* Click the button and fill out the on-screen registration form.

Important: There is no free discount code for Mastering the Art. The code supplied in the back of this book is applicable only to the Illustrator Fundamentals course.

That's it! Once you've registered, you can start learning immediately. Be sure to read the Orientation and Setup sections before starting the course so you can get the most out of the DigitalThink learning experience. If you have any questions, or if you need help with the course registration process, send email to illustrator@digitalthink.com.

System requirements

Classroom in a Book can be used on a Macintosh or on a PC that runs Windows. In addition to the system requirements for either system, you need the Adobe Illustrator 7.0 program and a CD-ROM drive to use the Classroom in a Book files.

Macintosh system requirements

To use Adobe Illustrator, you need the following hardware and software:

• An Apple® Macintosh computer with a 68030 processor (or later model) or a Power Macintosh

• At least 12 MB of random-access memory (RAM) available for the application, with a total of 16 MB of RAM for the system. To run the DigitalThink online companion course with Illustrator, you need 20 to 24 MB RAM.

• Apple System software 7.5 or later

• A CD-ROM drive

For the best performance, Adobe Systems recommends the following hardware and software:

• At least 32 MB of RAM

• ColorSync 2.1.1

Windows system requirements

To use Adobe Illustrator, you need the following hardware and software:

• An Intel® 80486 or faster processor

• Microsoft Windows 95 or Intel-based Windows NT™ version 4.0 or later

• At least 16 MB of RAM

• A CD-ROM drive

For the best performance, Adobe Systems recommends the following hardware and software:

• A Pentium®- or Pentium Pro-based or faster PC

• At least 32 MB of RAM

Adobe Illustrator performance improves with more RAM, a faster CPU, and a faster hard disk drive.

Getting started

To get started with Adobe Illustrator Classroom in a Book, you must install the Adobe Illustrator program, install the Acrobat Reader® program to view the movies and read additional information on the CD about Adobe products and services, and copy the Classroom in a Book lesson and sample files to your hard drive.

Installing the Adobe Illustrator program

If you haven't already done so, install the Adobe Illustrator program now. For complete instructions on installing Adobe Illustrator, see the *Adobe Illustrator Getting Started Guide* that comes with the program.

If you've never used Illustrator before, it may be helpful to first go through the Tour in the first chapter of the *Adobe Illustrator User Guide*. For an overview of what you can do with Illustrator, watch the 5-minute tour movie on the Adobe Illustrator Tour and Training CD. You must install the Acrobat Reader program to be able to view the movie.

Installing the Acrobat Reader program

Viewing and the movies and browsing the additional information on Adobe products and services like the *Adobe Electronic Printing Guide* requires that you install the Acrobat Reader® program. To install the software, use the instructions that correspond to your computer system, either the Macintosh or Windows.

To view and browse the PDF files on the *Adobe Illustrator Classroom in a CD*, you must have Acrobat Reader installed. To install the software, follow the instructions for your Macintosh or Windows computer.

To install the Adobe Acrobat program files on a Macintosh computer:

1 Insert the Adobe Acrobat for Macintosh CD into your CD-ROM drive.

2 Double-click the Install Adobe Acrobat 3.0 icon.

3 Click Continue in the Adobe Acrobat Installer dialog box.

4 Click Accept to accept the license agreement.

5 From the pop-up menu in the Install Adobe Acrobat dialog box, choose how to install the Adobe Acrobat program:

• Easy Install to install Acrobat Distiller®, Exchange, PDF Writer, Catalog, and several plug-ins in the Adobe Acrobat folder on your destination disk.

• Custom Install to select individual items for installation, and select the items you want to install.

6 Select a location for the installation; to select a new location, click the Select Folder button.

7 Click Install, and follow the on-screen instructions. When installation is complete, a message appears stating that the installation was successful.

8 Click Restart to restart your computer.

To install Adobe Acrobat in Windows:

1 Restart Windows and do not start any other applications.

2 Insert the Adobe Acrobat for Windows CD into your CD-ROM drive.

3 Follow the instructions for your platform:

• In Windows 3.1 or later and for Windows NT 3.5.1, from the Program Manager, choose File > Run.

• In Windows 95 or Windows NT 4.0, choose Start > Run.

4 Type **d:\Setup.exe** (where **d:** is the CD-ROM drive indicator); click OK.

5 Follow the instructions on-screen to progress through the introduction, and accept the license agreement

6 Choose a location for the installation: Accept the default target drive and folder displayed in the Destination Directory box, or click Browse and type a folder, a new drive, or both.

Note: Click the Disk Space button to display available disk space information about available hard drives.

7 Click Next. A message appears when installation is complete.

8 Click Finish; then click OK to complete the setup.

9 To start Acrobat Reader, double-click the application icon.

Copying the Classroom in a Book files

The Classroom in a Book CD-ROM disc includes folders containing all the electronic files for the Classroom in a Book lessons. Each lesson has its own folder. You must install these folders on your hard disk to use the files for the lessons. To save room on your hard disk, you can install the folder for each lesson as you need it.

To install the Classroom in a Book folders on the Macintosh:

1 Create a folder on your hard disk and name it AICIB.

2 Drag the Lessons folder from the *Adobe Illustrator Classroom in a Book* CD into the AICIB folder.

3 Drag the Samples folder from the *Adobe Illustrator Classroom in a Book* CD into the AICIB folder.

To install the Classroom in a Book files in Windows:

1 Insert the *Adobe Illustrator Classroom in a Book* CD into your CD-ROM drive.

2 Create a subdirectory on your hard disk and name it AICIB.

3 Copy the Lessons folder into the AICIB subdirectory.

4 Copy the Samples folder into the AICIB subdirectory.

Restoring default preferences

The preferences file controls how palettes and command settings appear on your screen when you open the Adobe Illustrator program. Each time you quit Adobe Illustrator, the position of the palettes and certain command settings are recorded in the Preferences file. If you want to restore the tools and palettes to their original settings, you can delete the Adobe Illustrator 7.0 Prefs file.

To quickly locate and delete the Adobe Illustrator preferences file, create an alias (Macintosh) or a shortcut (Windows) for the Preferences folder.

To delete the Illustrator preferences file on the Macintosh:

1 Locate the Adobe Illustrator 7.0 Prefs file in the Preferences folder in the System folder.

If you can't find the file, choose Find from the desktop File menu, type **Adobe Illustrator 7.0** in the text box, and click Find.

Note: If you still can't find the file, you probably haven't started Adobe Illustrator for the first time yet. The preferences file is created when you start the program.

2 Drag the Adobe Illustrator 7.0 Prefs file to the Trash.

3 Choose Special > Empty Trash.

To delete the Illustrator preferences file in Windows:

Delete the AIPrefs file in your Illustrator 7.0 directory.

Important: If you want to save the current settings, rename the Prefs file rather than throwing it away. When you are ready to restore the settings, change the name back to Adobe Illustrator 7.0 Prefs (Macintosh) or AIPrefs (Windows) and make sure that the file is located in the Preferences folder (Macintosh) or the Illustrator 7.0 directory (Windows).

Other resources

Classroom in a Book is not meant to replace documentation that comes with Adobe Illustrator. Only the commands and options used in the lessons are described in this book.

For comprehensive information about all of the program's features, refer to the *Adobe Illustrator User Guide* or to the Adobe Illustrator online help. You will also find the Quick Reference Card packaged with Adobe Illustrator a useful companion as you work through the lessons in this book. An online version of the Quick Reference Card is included in the online help.

About Adobe products and services

More information about Adobe products and services is available through the following:

• Forums on CompuServe and America Online. Forums and availability may vary by country.

• The Adobe home page on the World Wide Web. To open the Adobe home page, go to http://www.adobe.com.

• From Adobe's home page, you can choose Sales & Customer Support to select from a variety of support options, including the Technical Solutions Database, which provides information about all of Adobe's products.

• Adobe's own technical support bulletin-board system. To use the Adobe bulletin board, call 206-623-6984.

• FaxYI, a free fax-based service that provides the latest technical information about Adobe products. To use FaxYI, call 206-628-5737. This service is available 24 hours a day, seven days a week.

• The Adobe Certified Expert ™ (ACE) program, designed to validate an expert skill level of Adobe Illustrator 7.0. Careful testing of candidates ensures that each ACE has demonstrated expert product knowledge of the current release of Adobe Illustrator, resulting in increased marketability and an added credential.

Training for the ACE program is available through Adobe Authorized Learning Providers (AALP) and self-study. For more information about this program, send e-mail to certification@adobe.com or visit the Adobe Web site at http://www.adobe.com.

Fundamentals

In this section

Adobe Illustrator Fundamentals includes all you need to get up and running with Adobe Illustrator. After going through the Fundamentals, you'll know how to do the following:

- Navigate your way around the work area
- Draw basic shapes and use the pen tool for precision drawing
- Select and edit objects
- Use Illustrator painting tools and palettes
- Create and format display type and text columns
- Use layers to organize, edit, and display your artwork

The online course

The Web-based companion course from DigitalThink, *Illustrator Fundamentals*, is included free with this book. *Illustrator Fundamentals* offers more than 20 new lessons on the following topics:

- Module 1: Coming to Terms with Illustrator
- Module 2: Drawing and Modifying Basic Shapes
- Module 3: Coloring Shapes
- Module 4: Working in a Bézier World
- Module 5: Adding Type

See page 3 for information on how to log in to the course.

Lesson 1
The Illustrator Work Area

To make the best use of the extensive draw-ing, painting, and editing capabilities in Adobe Illustrator, it's important to learn how to navigate the work area. The work area consists of the artboard, the scratch area, the toolbox, and the default set of floating palettes.

In this lesson, you'll learn how to do the following:

• Open an Adobe Illustrator document

• Identify the page boundary of a document and the area of a page on which artwork can be printed, called *imageable* area

• View artwork in two ways. (Preview view shows all the painted characteristics of the artwork; Artwork view displays only outlines of the artwork.)

• Use viewing commands and tools to enlarge and reduce the display of artwork

• Work with palettes

• Save a document

Starting the Adobe Illustrator program

Double-click the Adobe Illustrator icon to start the program.

When you start Adobe Illustrator, an untitled document window, the menu bar, the toolbox, and three palette groups appear on-screen.

Adobe Illustrator Classroom in a Book comes with a free online companion course, Illustrator Fundamentals. For information on how to log in to the course, see page 3. If you've already logged in, get started by reading the course orientation and the introduction to Module 1.

About Adobe Illustrator graphics

Adobe Illustrator creates vector graphics. Vector graphics consist of lines and curves defined by mathematical objects called *vectors*. For example, when you draw a 1-inch circle in a vector-based program, such as Adobe Illustrator, the program creates the circle based on its shape and size. You can then move, scale, or change the color of the circle without affecting the quality of the graphic.

Opening the work file

You'll start by opening a finished piece of artwork and use viewing commands and tools to change the display of the artwork.

1 Choose File > Open. Locate and open the Bttrfly.ai file in the Lesson01 folder. This folder is located in the Lessons folder within the AICIB folder on your hard drive.

(To see a sample of the finished artwork, open the Bttrfly2.ai file in the Lesson01 folder, inside the Samples folder in the AICIB folder on your hard drive.)

2 Choose File > Save As, name the file Bttrfly1.ai; then click Save.

Identifying the page boundary

When you open a document for the first time in Adobe Illustrator, an outline, called the *artboard*, appears in the center of the document window. The size and orientation of the artboard is determined by the settings in the Document Setup dialog box. By default, the size is 8-1/2-inches by 11 inches, and the orientation is vertical. You can change these parameters, which you'll do in a later lesson.

The dotted line within the artboard identifies the *imageable* area. Any artwork within the dotted line can be printed.

The area between the dotted line and the edge of the artboard represents the non-imageable area; any artwork between these lines cannot be printed.

The area surrounding the artboard can be thought of as a scratch area. You can move objects onto the scratch area for later use, but it's a good idea to delete them before you prepare your artwork for final output. While objects in the scratch area do not print, they do add to the size of the Illustrator file.

A. *Imageable area*
B. *Nonimageable area*
C. *Artboard* D. *Scratch area*

Viewing artwork

When you open a file, it is displayed in Preview view, which displays artwork the way it will print. When you're working with large or complex illustrations, you may want to view only the outlines, or *wireframes*, of objects in your artwork, so that the screen doesn't have to redraw the artwork each time you make a change.

1 Choose View > Artwork. Only the outlines of the objects are displayed.

2 Choose View > Preview to see all the attributes of the artwork.

Artwork view   *Preview view*

Using the Illustrator toolbox

The Illustrator toolbox contains selection tools, drawing and painting tools, editing tools, viewing tools, and the Fill and Stroke color selection boxes. As you work through the lessons, you'll learn about each tool's specific function.

Identifying tools

Because the toolbox contains many tools, it can be difficult to remember the name of each tool when you're first getting started with Illustrator. You can display the name of each tool and its single-letter keyboard shortcut by positioning the pointer over the tool.

Try positioning the pointer over a few different tools. You don't need to click a tool to see its name; position the pointer over the tool for a few seconds and the tool name will appear.

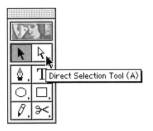

Selecting tools

To select a tool, you can either click the tool in the toolbox or press the tool's keyboard shortcut. For example, you can press V to select the selection tool from the keyboard. Selected tools remain active until you click a different tool or press another keyboard shortcut.

Practice selecting tools in the toolbox using both methods. Once you've selected a tool, its name is displayed at the bottom of the artwork window.

Some of the tools in the toolbox contain a small triangle at the bottom right corner, indicating the presence of additional hidden tools.

You can select hidden tools in either of the following ways:

• Move the mouse pointer to a tool and hold down the mouse button; then drag to the desired tool.

• Press the tool's keyboard shortcut repeatedly until the tool you want is displayed.

Note: If you click a screen display option at the bottom of the toolbox to change the way your artwork is displayed on-screen, be sure to click the Standard screen mode to return to the default work area view.

The ellipse tool in Illustrator functions a bit differently from the similar tools you may already know. For more practice with the ellipse tool and with other Illustrator drawing tools, see the "Simple shapes" and "Straight lines" lessons in Module 1 of the online companion course.

Changing the view of artwork

You can reduce or enlarge the view of artwork at any magnification level from 6.25% to 1600%. Adobe Illustrator displays the percentage of the artwork's actual size in the title bar, next to the filename, and at the lower left corner of the Adobe Illustrator window. When you use any of the viewing tools and commands, note that only the display of the artwork is affected, and not the actual size of the artwork.

Using the View commands

Each time you choose a Zoom command, the view of the artwork is resized. Additional viewing options appear at the lower left corner of the window in a hidden menu, indicated by a a triangle next to the percentage.

1 To enlarge or reduce the view of artwork using the View menu, do one of the following:

• Choose View > Zoom In to enlarge the display of the Work01 artwork.

• Choose View > Zoom Out to reduce the view of the Work01 artwork.

• Move the mouse pointer onto the view indicator at the lower left corner of the document window; then drag to a new view.

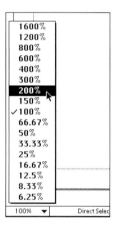

If you've selected a level of magnification over 100%, you may not be able to see all of your artwork in the document window. You can use the Fit in Window command to display all the artwork at a reduced view.

2 Choose View > Fit in Window. A reduced view of the entire document is displayed in the window.

3 To display artwork at actual size, choose View > Actual Size. The artwork is displayed at 100%. (The actual size of your artwork determines how much of it can be viewed on-screen at 100%.)

4 Choose View > Fit in Window before continuing to the next section.

Using the zoom tool

In addition to the View commands, you can use the zoom tool to magnify and reduce the view of artwork.

1 Click the zoom tool (🔍) in the toolbox to select it, and move the tool pointer into the document window. Notice that a plus sign appears at the center of the zoom tool.

2 Position the zoom tool over the butterfly at the top of the illustration and click once. The artwork is displayed at 66.67%.

3 Click the zoom tool two more times over the top butterfly. The view is increased to 150%, and you'll notice that the area you clicked is magnified. Next, you'll reduce the view of the artwork using the zoom-out tool.

4 With the zoom tool still selected, position the pointer over the top butterfly and hold down Option (Macintosh) or Alt (Windows). A minus sign appears at the center of the zoom tool (🔍).

5 Click the zoom-out tool twice; the view of the artwork is reduced to 66.67%.

In addition to clicking the zoom tools, you can drag a marquee to magnify a specific area of your artwork.

6 Drag a marquee around the lower butterfly.

The percentage at which the area is magnified is determined by the size of the marquee you draw with the zoom tool (the smaller the marquee, the larger the level of magnification).

Area selected   *Resulting view*

Note: *Although you can draw a marquee with the zoom-in tool to enlarge the view of artwork, you cannot draw a marquee with the zoom-out tool to reduce the view of artwork.*

You can also use the zoom tool to return to a 100% view of your artwork, regardless of the current magnification level.

7 Double-click the zoom tool in the toolbox to return to a 100% view.

Because the zoom tool is used frequently during the editing process to enlarge and reduce the view of artwork, you can select it from the keyboard at any time without deselecting any other tool you may be using.

8 Before selecting the zoom tool from the keyboard, click any other tool in the toolbox and move it into the document window.

9 Now, hold down Spacebar+Command (Macintosh) or Spacebar+Ctrl (Windows) to select the zoom tool from the keyboard. Zoom in on any area of the artwork, and then release the keys. The tool you selected in the previous step is displayed.

10 To select the zoom-out tool from the keyboard, hold down Spacebar+Command+Option (Macintosh) or Spacebar+Ctrl+Alt (Windows). Click the desired area to reduce the view of the artwork, and then release the keys.

11 Double-click the zoom tool in the toolbox to return to a 100% view of your artwork.

Scrolling through a document

You use the hand tool to scroll to different areas of a document.

1 Click the hand tool in the toolbox.

2 Drag downward in the document window. As you drag, the artwork moves with the hand.

As with the zoom tool, you can select the hand tool from the keyboard without deselecting the active tool.

3 Before selecting the hand tool from the keyboard, click any other tool in the toolbox and move it into the document window.

4 Hold down the Spacebar to select the hand tool from the keyboard, and then drag to bring the artwork back into view.

You can also use the hand tool as a shortcut to fit all the artwork in the window.

5 Double-click the hand tool to fit the document in the window.

Working with palettes

Multiple tabs in a palette indicate a palette group. By default, the Illustrator palettes are arranged in three groups, stacked along the right side of the window.

• The Info/Transform/Align group

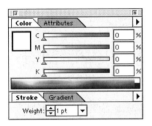

• The Color/Attributes/Stroke/Gradient group

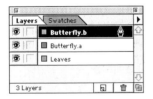

• The Layers/Swatches palette group

Selecting palettes

To use a palette, you must click its tab to bring it to the front of the group before you can select any of its options.

Click a palette tab, for example, Transform.

Hiding palettes

You can hide palettes you're not using by clicking the close box in the palette. On the Macintosh, the close box is at the top left corner of the palette; in Windows, the close box is at the top right corner of the palette.

1 Click the close box to hide the Layers/Swatches palette group.

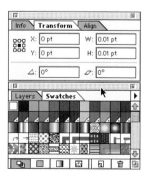

To display a palette after it's been hidden, use the Window menu.

2 Choose Window > Show Layers to redisplay the Layers/Swatches palette group.

You can hide all the open palettes and the toolbox with a single keystroke.

3 Press Tab to hide all the open palettes and the toolbox; then press Tab again to redisplay the palettes and the toolbox.

Moving palettes

All the Illustrator palettes are *floating*—that is, they always appear in front of any artwork you have on-screen, so that you can move the palettes to see more of your artwork. To move a palette anywhere on the screen, drag its title bar.

Drag the title bar of one of the palettes to move it on your screen.

Now, drag the palette by its title bar to position it under another palette. Notice that the palette group snaps to an invisible grid to align it with the other palette.

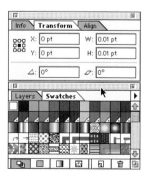

Selecting palette options

Some palettes have menus, from which you can select additional options.

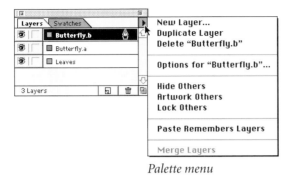

Palette menu

1 Click the Layers palette tab.

2 Click the black triangle at the right of the Layers palette to display the Layers menu.

3 Release the mouse button (Macintosh) or press Esc (Windows) to close the menu without selecting a command.

Collapsing a palette

All palettes are *collapsible*. When a palette is collapsed, only its title bar and palette tabs are visible, thereby increasing your workspace.

Choose either of the following methods to collapse a palette:

• Click the minimize box in the right corner of the palette's title bar. (In Windows, click the box containing the horizontal line, not the box containing the *x*.) The palette group collapses. Click the box again to expand the palette.

• Double-click the palette tab; the palette group collapses. Double-click the palette tab again; the palette expands to its full default size.

Note: If you accidentally close a palette, use the Window menu to reopen the desired palette.

Resizing a palette

You can resize some of the palettes using the size box in the lower right corner of the palette.

1 Click the Swatches palette tab; then drag the lower right corner of the palette to the right about 1 inch. The color swatches are redistributed in the Swatches palette.

2 Click the minimize box in the upper right corner of the Swatches palette to return it to its default size.

Note: If you've resized a palette, you must click the minimize box twice to collapse it. The first click returns the palette to its default size; the second click collapses it.

Customizing palettes

Palette groups can be separated and reorganized. If you have a small screen, you may want to put all the palettes you use into a single group. If you have a larger screen, you may want to separate certain palettes from their groups.

1 Drag the Swatches palette tab outside its palette group.

As you drag the pointer outside the palette group, a gray outline appears.

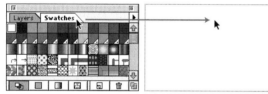

Select the palette tab.   *Drag the palette to a new location.*

2 Release the mouse button when the gray outline appears. The Swatches palette is separated from Layers/Swatches palette group.

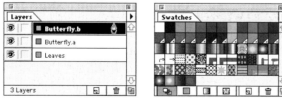

Separated palettes

To combine palettes, drag a palette by its tab onto another group of palettes.

3 Drag the Swatches palette tab onto the Color/Attributes/Stroke/Gradient palette group. The Swatches palette is added to the palette group.

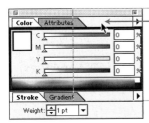 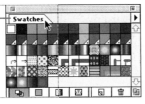

Select the palette tab.   *Drag the palette to another group.*

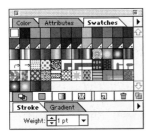

Merged palettes

4 Drag the Swatches palette tab back to the Layers palette.

Resetting palettes

To reset palettes to their default palette group settings, you must delete the Preferences file. For step-by-step instructions on how to delete the preferences file, see "Restoring default preferences" on page 7.

Choose File > Close, save your changes if prompted, and close the file.

Using shortcuts

Now that you've learned the basics about how to move around the Illustrator work area, you may want to begin using some of the keyboard shortcuts that appear to the right of the commands in the menus. These are especially useful for operations you perform frequently, such as displaying a specific command's dialog box.

Review

• Name two ways to select a tool from the toolbox.

Click the tool in the toolbox, or press the tool's keyboard equivalent.

• Name two ways to select hidden tools from the toolbox.

Hold down the mouse button to display the hidden tools palette and then drag to the tool you want, or press the keyboard equivalent of a tool repeatedly until the hidden tool becomes active.

• Name three ways to change the view (display) of artwork.

Use the hand tool to scroll to different parts of the artwork, use the zoom-in and zoom-out tools to magnify and reduce the view of the artwork, or select the view you want from the View menu.

• How do you select the hand tool and the zoom tool from the keyboard without deselecting the active tool?

To select the hand tool from the keyboard, hold down the Spacebar. To select the zoom tool from the keyboard, hold down Spacebar+Command (Macintosh) or Spacebar+Ctrl (Windows).

• How do you display a palette once it's hidden?

Choose the desired Show command from the Window menu.

Lesson 2

Lesson 2

Making Selections

Learning to make selections is of primary importance in Adobe Illustrator, because you must first select what you want to affect. Adobe Illustrator has three selection tools: the selection tool, which selects entire objects; the direct-selection tool, which selects portions, or segments, of objects; and the group-selection tool, which selects a single object within a set of objects you have defined as a group.

In this lesson, you'll learn how to do the following:

• Use the selection tool to select entire objects and type

• Switch between Preview and Artwork view to see the paint attributes and wire-frame view of an object, respectively

• Select and edit portions, or segments, of objects using the direct-selection tool

• Group objects into a set

Get comfortable with the arrow tools by practicing selecting entire shapes and individual points in "The arrow tools" lesson in Module 1 of the online companion course.

Selecting objects

Before you can modify an object, you must distinguish it from the objects around it. You do that by selecting the object with one of the selection tools.

You'll start the lesson by selecting the wings of the swan. You'll use the selection tool, which lets you select entire objects.

1 Choose File > Open, and locate and open the Select.ai file in the Lesson02 folder. This folder is inside the Lessons folder of the AICIB folder on your hard drive.

(To see a sample of the finished artwork, open the Select2.ai file in the Lesson02 folder, inside the Samples folder in the AICIB folder on your hard drive.)

2 Choose File > Save As, name the file Select01.ai; then click Save.

3 Click the selection tool (➤) in the toolbox, and then click the outline of the swan.

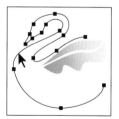

When an object is selected, its outline and points, called *anchor points*, appear highlighted.

Anchor points define where each segment of a path starts and ends; that is, they anchor the path in place. By moving anchor points, you modify path segments and change the shape of a path.

4 Click within the filled area of either wing. The entire object is selected.

You can change this default behavior if you don't want clicking anywhere within a filled area to select the object—for example, if you're working with overlapping filled objects. To change the default, you turn off the Area Select option in the General Preferences dialog box. When the Area Select option is turned off, you must click the outline of an object to select it. (To display the dialog box, choose File > Preferences > General.)

Now you'll continue to select the swan.

5 Hold down the Shift key and click the remaining wing; both wings are selected. To extend a selection, you hold down Shift and click additional objects.

You deselect objects when you no longer want to edit them.

6 Deselect the wings using one of the following deselection methods:

• Click away from the object anywhere in the window.

• Choose Edit > Deselect All.

You can also select objects by dragging with the selection tool.

7 Drag the selection tool so that the marquee contains at least a portion of every object in the swan.

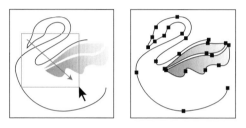

8 Deselect the swan by clicking away from it anywhere in the window or by choosing Edit > Deselect All.

You've been working in Preview view, the default view of a document, which lets you see how objects are painted. Sometimes the paint attributes can be distracting, however, and you may want to work with just the wireframe view of an object.

9 Choose View > Artwork.

To select any object in Artwork view, you click its outline.

10 Using the selection tool, click different parts of the illustration; then deselect the artwork.

Selecting parts of an object

Next you'll select part of the outline of the swan, and adjust its shape. To select and edit individual segments of an object, you use the direct-selection tool.

1 Click the direct-selection tool (⬀) in the toolbox. Then click the lower left edge of the swan.

The anchor points on the segment appear as hollow squares, indicating that you have selected the segment without selecting the anchor points. In addition, *direction lines* emanate from the anchor points because the segment is curved. You can drag the direction lines' endpoints, called *direction points,* to control the angle of a curve.

2 Drag the segment to see how it moves independently from the anchor points.

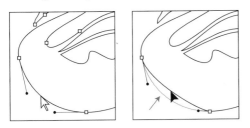

3 Now drag the bottommost anchor point upward to adjust the curve of the swan.

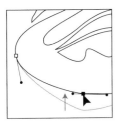

To adjust a curved segment, you move the segment between the points anchoring it, or you move one or more of its anchor or direction points.

4 Drag the direction point (the filled blue circle) at the left edge of the swan down and to the left to adjust the curve.

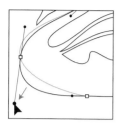

If you make a mistake as you drag, you can undo your work by choosing Edit > Undo. Adobe Illustrator lets you undo a series of actions—limited only by your computer's memory—by repeatedly choosing Edit > Undo. (To set the minimum number of undos, choose File > Preferences > Units and Undo.)

You can also adjust more than one segment of an object by selecting multiple anchor points.

5 With the direct-selection tool (⬚), click the edge of the lower wing to display the anchor points, and then click the anchor point near the scallop on the left of the wing. Shift-click the two points to the right to select those anchor points as well.

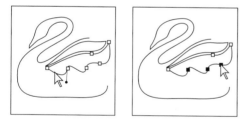

You use the same technique of Shift-clicking to extend a selection using the other selection tools.

6 Now drag any part of the segment downward to expand the lower portion of the wing.

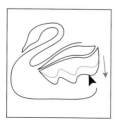

Note that the entire lower segment between the two hollow anchor points is selected and adjusted.

You can also select segments by dragging over specific anchor points with the direct-selection tool.

7 Deselect the artwork by clicking away from it anywhere in the window.

Now you'll adjust the length of both wings.

8 Drag over the anchor points at the tips of the wings, and then drag either anchor point to the right to lengthen both wings.

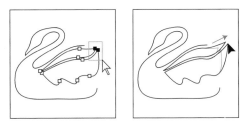

9 Choose View > Preview to see the swan with all the attributes. You can also choose Command+Y (Macintosh) or Ctrl+Y (Windows) to switch between Preview and Artwork view.

Selecting an object within a set of objects

Now you will group the two wave shapes in the artwork. Grouping a set of objects lets you select and modify the objects as a single unit.

1 Click the selection tool (↖) in the toolbox.

Note: When the direct-selection tool is selected, you can switch to the selection tool by pressing Command+Tab (Macintosh) or Ctrl+Tab (Windows).

2 Click the top wave, and then Shift-click the bottom wave.

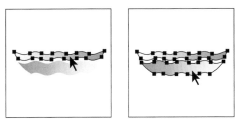

Shift-click to extend a selection.

3 Choose Object > Group.

4 Deselect the artwork by clicking away from it anywhere in the window.

When you combine several objects into a group, you can manipulate the objects as a single unit when you use the selection tool and the transformation tools. You can then move or transform a number of objects without affecting their individual positions or attributes.

5 With the selection tool still active, click either wave to select the group.

6 Drag the group so that it intersects with the outline of the swan.

The selection tool you choose to use with grouped objects determines what is selected. Consider these guidelines:

• Once objects have been grouped, selecting any part of the group with the selection tool selects the entire group. If you are unsure whether an object is part of a group, select it with the selection tool (↖).

• If you want to select and adjust an object or single path within a group without ungrouping all of the objects, use the direct-selection tool (↖).

• If you have groups of objects within other groups, you can select the next group in the grouping hierarchy using the group-selection tool (↖⁺).

For more information about using the group-selection tool, and creating and manipulating groups of objects, see "Grouping and ungrouping objects" in Chapter 6 of the *Adobe Illustrator User Guide* or in online Help.

 You can align type and other objects easily using the Adobe Illustrator grid. Take "The grid" lesson in Module 1 of the online companion course to learn how.

Selecting type

Next, you will edit the *swan* text and then drag it into place on the illustration.

1 Click the type tool (**T**) in the toolbox.

The type tool's I-beam pointer lets you select individual characters, words, and paragraphs, and then change the type attributes or edit the text.

2 To select type to edit the text, do one of the following:

• Position the I-beam pointer where the text starts and drag to the end of the text.

• Click the type with the type tool, and then choose Edit > Select All.

• Double-click the text to select a word. (To select a paragraph, position the I-beam pointer in the text and triple-click.)

3 Edit the text by typing **cygnet** on the keyboard.

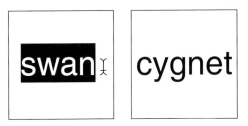

When you want to select all of the type on a path or in a type container, you use the selection tool on the path or type container—just as you would select an object.

4 Click the selection tool (➤) in the toolbox to select the type and display its anchor point and *baseline* (the line on which the type rests).

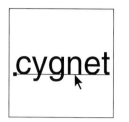

5 Drag either the anchor point or the baseline to move the cygnet text into position on the right side of the artwork.

To select type for manipulating—for example, to move, rotate, or scale type—you select the type with the selection tool. (If the default Area Select option in the General Preferences dialog box is turned off, you must click the type baseline with the selection tool to select the type. To display the dialog box, choose File > Preferences > General.)

For more information on creating and editing type, see "Using Type" (Chapter 13) of the *Adobe Illustrator User Guide* or in online Help.

Now you will drag the finished artwork to the top left of the document.

6 Choose Edit > Select All to select the entire artwork.

7 Drag any of the anchor points, filled areas, or curves to move the artwork to the top left.

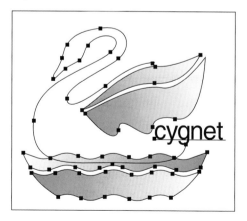

8 Choose File > Close to close the Select01.ai file. If desired, save your changes.

This completes the selecting lesson. You'll have many opportunities in the upcoming lessons to practice the techniques you've just learned.

Review

• What is the purpose of each of the three selection tools?

The selection tool (➤) selects entire objects. The direct-selection tool (➤) selects portions, or segments, of objects. The group-selection tool (➤⁺)selects a single object within a set of objects you have defined as a group.

• How can you add to a selection to include more than the original selection?

With a selection tool active, Shift-click objects that you want to add to the selection.

• How do you select just part of an object?

You use the direct-selection tool to select just part of an object.

• What selection tool do you use to adjust a curved segment? How do you adjust the segment?

You use the direct-selection tool to adjust a curved segment. You can drag the segment's direction point, anchor point, or the entire segment to adjust it.

• Why might you group objects? Give an example of when you would group artwork.

Grouping a set of objects lets you select and modify the objects as a single unit. You might group several objects such as the shapes forming a company logo and name, to use them together.

• How do you select a line of type when you want to edit the letters or change the attributes (color, font, size, and so on) of individual letters and words?

Use one of these techniques to select a line of type: (1) Position the type tool's I-beam pointer where the text starts and drag to the end of the text. (2) Click the text with the type tool, and then choose Edit > Select All. (3) Double-click the text to select a word. (4) To select a paragraph, position the type tool's I-beam pointer in the text and triple-click.

• How do you select type when you want to scale or rotate it?

To select type for manipulating—for example, to move, rotate, or scale type—you select the type baseline with the selection tool.

Lesson 3

Lesson 3

Creating Basic Shapes

Many objects in Adobe Illustrator can be created by starting with basic shapes and then editing them to create new shapes. For example, you can use tools to create polygons, stars, and spirals, and then combine these shapes to build more complex objects. In this lesson, you will create some shapes and then modify them to create portions of the television artwork.

In this lesson, you'll learn how to do the following:

• Use tools and commands to create basic shapes

• Duplicate and combine objects to create new shapes

• Use selection tools to select objects and parts of objects

• Paint objects

Using the tools

To begin working, you'll create a new document. When you start Adobe Illustrator, the program automatically opens a new document. You can also create a new document at any time once Illustrator is running.

1 Choose File > New to open a new document.

(To see a sample of the finished artwork, open the Shapes2.ai file in the Lesson03 folder, inside the Samples folder in the AICIB folder on your hard drive.)

The new document appears with the name "Untitled art" in its title bar, and the toolbox appears on the left side of the screen. You'll begin creating artwork using a tool in the toolbox.

2 In the toolbox, click the Default Fill and Stroke button to set the paint attributes to their defaults.

In Adobe Illustrator, you control the thickness and color of lines that you draw by setting *stroke attributes*. A *stroke* is the paint characteristics of a line. A *fill* is the paint characteristics of an object. The default settings will let you see the objects you draw in white with a black outline.

3 Position the pointer on the ellipse tool in the toolbox, and drag to the right to select the star tool.

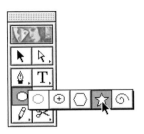

Note: *The star, spiral, and polygon tools are optional tools that come with the Adobe Illustrator program. If the star tool doesn't appear in the toolbox, use the Custom option of the Adobe Illustrator Installer to select and install the Plug-ins folder.*

The star creates a star-shaped object with a given number of points and size. You can create a star by dragging, or you can specify its dimensions.

4 Drag in the artwork window to draw a star. By default, the star tool draws a 5-pointed star.

5 Press Delete to delete your drawing.

You'll draw the star again and use some keystrokes to control its shape.

6 Drag in the artwork window again to draw another star, but do not release the mouse button.

As you drag, choose any of the following options to control the star's shape:

• To add or subtract points from the star, press the Up Arrow key or the Down Arrow key before releasing the mouse button. The tool stays set to the last value you set, until you reset the number.

• To rotate the star, drag the pointer in an arc.

- To keep the star's top point pointing up, hold down Shift.

- To keep the sides of the star straight, hold down Option (Macintosh) or Alt (Windows).

- To keep the inner radius constant, hold down Control.

- To move the star as you draw it, hold down the Spacebar.

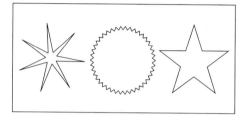

Now you will create the television knobs.

7 Position the pointer on the star tool in the toolbox, and drag to the right to select the polygon tool (○).

This tool lets you create a symmetrical *polygon*—a many-sided object.

8 Drag to draw a polygon, pressing Shift to constrain its sides.

By default, the polygon tool draws an octagon. As with the star tool, you can use similar keystrokes with the polygon tool to control the shape of the polygon.

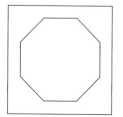

Next, you'll display a center point for use when aligning objects.

9 Choose Window > Show Attributes to display the Attributes palette. Select the Show Center Point button to display the polygon's center point.

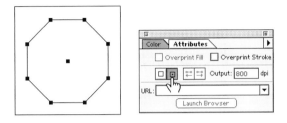

All objects created with one of the shape tools have a center point. The center point is visible as long as the object is selected. You can use this point to drag the object or to align the object with other elements in your artwork. You can make the center point visible or invisible, but you cannot delete it.

10 Position the pointer on the polygon tool in the toolbox, and drag to the right to select the centered-ellipse tool (⊙).

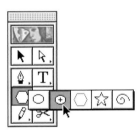

11 Position the pointer over the center point of the polygon.

12 Hold down Shift; then drag outward from the center point of the polygon to draw a circle. As you begin dragging, the pointer becomes hollow, indicating that the pointer is aligned with the center of the polygon.

Holding down Shift as you drag with an ellipse tool constrains the shape of the object to a circle. Holding down Shift as you drag with a rectangle tool constrains the shape of the object to a square.

Learn more about how to create and reshape geometric objects to make free-form objects by taking the "Polygons, stars and spirals" and "Editing shapes" lessons in Module 2 of the online companion course.

Combining shapes

Now you'll combine the basic shapes that you just created, using a Pathfinder command. The circle should still be selected.

1 Click the selection tool (⭡) in the toolbox, and move the pointer over to the polygon.

2 Hold down Shift, and then click the polygon to add it to the selection of the circle. Shift-clicking an unselected object with a selection tool adds the object to a selection.

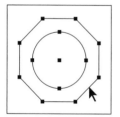

Next, you'll paint the shapes.

3 Click the Fill box in the toolbox.

4 Choose Window > Show Swatches if the Swatches palette is not visible. You use the Swatches palette to select and store colors.

5 Click a blue swatch in the Swatches palette to fill both objects with blue.

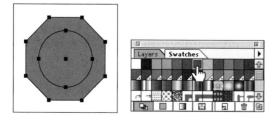

Now you'll use the Pathfinder > Exclude command to create a new shape by deleting areas that the two shapes have in common. The Pathfinder commands combine, isolate, and subdivide objects, as well as build new objects formed by the intersection of objects.

6 Choose Object > Pathfinder > Exclude to delete areas that are common to the selection.

The Exclude command traces all nonoverlapping areas of the selected objects, making the overlapping areas transparent.

7 Drag the polygon over another object to see that it has a hole in the center. Choose Edit > Undo to undo the move.

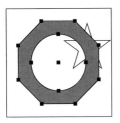

8 Click away from the artwork to deselect it.

Another way to create shapes is to combine them into a single shape using the Pathfinder > Unite option.

9 In the toolbox, click the Default Fill and Stroke button (or press D) to return the paint settings to their defaults.

10 Click the centered-ellipse tool (⊙) in the toolbox.

11 Position the pointer in the window, hold down Shift, and drag outward to draw the bottom of the vase.

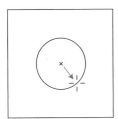
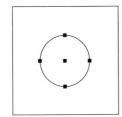

12 Click the rectangle tool (□) in the toolbox to select it, and position the pointer above the shape you just drew.

13 Drag downward to draw a tall, rectangular shape for the neck of the vase.

If necessary, use the selection tool to drag the shape into position. If you make a mistake, choose Edit > Undo and repeat the step.

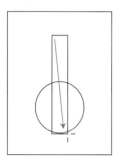

14 Click the selection tool (➤), and Shift-click the circle to select both shapes.

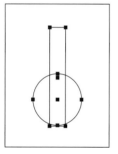

15 Now choose Object > Pathfinder > Unite to combine the shapes into a single shape.

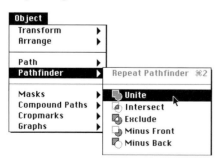

The Unite command traces the outline of all selected objects as if they were a single, merged object. Any objects inside the selected objects are deleted.

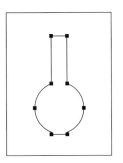

16 In the Swatches palette, click a radial gradient to fill the vase.

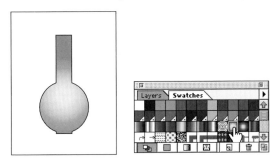

A *gradient fill* is a graduated blend between two or more colors or tints of the same color. A radial gradient changes colors starting from the center point of the fill and radiating outward to the endpoint. (For more information on gradients, see Lesson 19, "Creating and Editing a Gradient Fill.")

17 Deselect the shape by clicking away from the artwork.

Creating zigzag lines

Illustrator lets you draw lines in many ways. You'll start by setting a color to paint just the line.

1 In the toolbox, click the Fill box if it isn't already selected. Then click the None button in the toolbox (or press /) to change the current fill to None.

Now you'll create a zigzag line, starting from a straight horizontal line.

2 Select the pen tool (✒) in the toolbox.

3 Move the pointer to the window, and click it to create a starting point.

Clicking with the pen tool sets an anchor point and indicates that you are about to draw a straight line.

4 Shift-click a point about 3 inches from the starting point.

To draw straight lines with the pen tool, you click to create a starting point and an ending point. Shift-clicking constrains the line to multiples of 45° angles.

In Illustrator, points on paths are called *anchor points*. As their name implies, anchor points set the position of line segments. The line is painted with the current paint attributes—in this case, a stroke of black.

5 Command-click (Macintosh) or Ctrl-click (Windows) the line to select it.

The Command/Ctrl key activates the current selection tool, and clicking the path selects it.

Next, you'll make the line a zigzag.

6 Choose Filter > Distort > Zig Zag. (Choose the Distort command listed first in the Filter menu.)

7 In the Zig Zag dialog box, turn on the Preview option so that you can see the effect of your settings.

8 Enter 8 for the Amount and 5 for Ridges/inch. Select the Smooth Points option, and click OK.

Note: *If the Zig Zag filter produces straight, jagged lines instead of wavy zigzags, you can use the Round Corners filter to convert them to continuous curves.*

Duplicating objects

Another way to create shapes is by duplicating existing objects. Now you'll try out various ways to copy objects, using the Transform palette and menu commands.

1 If the line isn't selected, Command-click (Macintosh) or Ctrl-click (Windows) the line.

2 Choose Window > Show Transform to display the Transform palette.

3 In the Transform palette, position the pointer in the Y text box *after* the current value. The Y text box specifies the location of the reference point in relation to the *y* (vertical) axis.

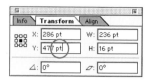

You can use the Transform palette to move, rotate, scale, skew, and resize selected objects. You can control where the transformation begins by clicking one of the boxes in the upper left of the palette that represent the object's bounding box. (The bounding box defines the selected artwork's boundaries.)

Now you'll move the line down 1/2-inch by performing a subtraction operation in the Transform palette.

4 Make sure that the pointer is inserted after the existing value; then type **–0.5 in** ; (*do not type a period after* "in"). Hold down Option (Macintosh) or Alt (Windows) and press Return or Enter to apply the value to the object.

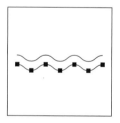

A copy of the line moves down 1/2-inch. Holding down Option/Alt as you press Return or Enter in the Transform palette creates a copy of the transformed object.

In Adobe Illustrator, you can enter values in text boxes in other than the preset unit. You can also add, subtract, multiply, divide, define percentages, and perform other mathematical operations in any Illustrator text box that accepts numeric values. Illustrator converts the values to the set unit, performs the calculation, and uses the result. For more information, see "Automatically converting unit values in text boxes" in Chapter 3 of the *Adobe Illustrator User Guide* or in online Help.

5 To repeat the move-and-copy operation, choose Object > Transform > Transform Again (Command+D on the Macintosh, or Ctrl+D in Windows). Continue pressing Command/Ctrl+D until you have created eight lines.

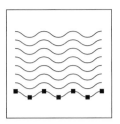

The Transform Again command lets you repeat a move, scale, rotate, reflect, or shear operation as many times as you want. You must choose the command immediately after you perform the operation.

Dividing shapes

Now you will create the outline for the TV screen. You'll divide overlapping shapes so that you can paint them individually.

1 Position the pointer on the rectangle tool (□) in the toolbox.

The rounded-rectangle tool draws squares and rectangles with rounded corners; you can set the size of the curve.

2 Drag to the right to select the rounded-rectangle tool (□).

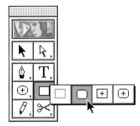

3 Position the pointer at the top left of the wavy lines, and drag to create the screen. If necessary, use the selection tool (▸) to drag the rounded rectangle to reposition it.

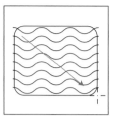

4 Click the selection tool (▸) in the toolbox, and drag to select all of the objects.

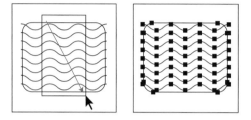

Notice that any line partially enclosed by the marquee becomes selected.

(For more information about selecting, see the "Making Selections" lesson and the "Drawing and Selecting" movie on the Adobe Illustrator Tour and Training CD.)

Now you'll use the Divide command to create the TV screen from the zigzag lines and rectangle.

5 Choose Object > Pathfinder > Divide to divide the selection of overlapping objects into discrete, closed shapes and eliminate stray artwork.

Notice how the shapes outside of the selection have been deleted.

The Divide command divides a piece of artwork into its component filled faces (a *face* is an area undivided by a line segment). The resulting faces can then be ungrouped and manipulated independently of each other.

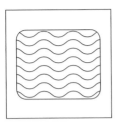

Note: You can have the Divide command remove unpainted artwork. For more information, see "Setting Pathfinder preferences" in Chapter 7 of the Adobe Illustrator User Guide *or in online Help.*

6 Click away from the artwork to deselect it.

 You can apply irregular changes to geometric shapes and turn stars into starfish! Learn how in the "Rotating and twirling shapes" lesson in Module 2 of the online companion course.

Editing individual segments

To complete the artwork, you'll select individual waves and paint them. Applying the Divide command *grouped* the waves. Grouping combines objects into a group so that the objects are treated as a single unit.

1 In the toolbox, click the Fill box.

2 To select an individual wave, position the pointer on the direct-selection tool(⬉) in the toolbox and drag to the right to select the group-selection tool (⬉⁺).

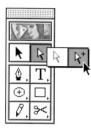

The group-selection tool lets you select objects within a group. (For more informa-tion about the group-selection tool, see "Selecting objects" in Chapter 5 of the *Adobe Illustrator User Guide* or in online Help.)

3 Click any wave outline to select it.

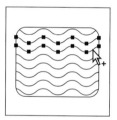

4 Specify a new color by doing one of the following:

• In the Swatches palette, click a color swatch.

• Choose Window > Show Color to display the Color palette, and then drag the color sliders. (Using the color sliders, you can edit the fill and stroke colors according to several different color models. You select a color model by pressing the black triangle in the palette to display the palette menu, and then choose a model from the palette menu.)

• In the Color palette, enter values next to the color sliders.

• In the toolbox, click the Gradient button. Then in the Swatches palette, click a gradient.

5 Repeat steps 3 and 4 to paint the rest of the waves.

6 Choose File > Close. If desired, name the file and save your changes.

You've completed the basic shapes lesson and created the television artwork.

For more information about selecting a fill or stroke color, see Lesson 4, "Painting," or see "Painting" (Chapter 9) in the *Adobe Illustrator User Guide* or in online Help.

Review

• How do you choose a selection tool without deselecting the active tool?

Press Command (Macintosh) or Ctrl (Windows), and click the object.

• Describe two ways to duplicate an object.

Select the object first. Then you can duplicate objects in many ways. (1) You can use the standard Macintosh and Windows commands of Edit > Copy and Edit > Paste. (2) You can select an object and then Option-drag or Alt-drag to copy it. (3) After using one of the first two methods to copy and paste, you can repeat the operation by choosing Transform > Transform Again or pressing Command+D (Macintosh) or Ctrl+D (Windows). (4) You can use the Transform palette to apply a change and duplicate the object simultaneously by pressing Option+Return (Macintosh) or Alt+Enter (Windows).

• Why is the number of anchor points on a line significant? How can you add anchor points to a line?

Anchor points divide a line into segments and let you control the shape of the line. You can use anchor points to edit these segments. You can add anchor points using the add-anchor-point tool.

• How do you create a hole in your artwork?

You can use the Object > Pathfinder > Exclude command to create a see-through object. You overlap two objects, and then apply the Exclude command; the topmost object will cut a hole through the backmost object.

• How do you select an object within a group?

You use the group-selection tool to select the object.

Lesson 4

Lesson 4

Painting

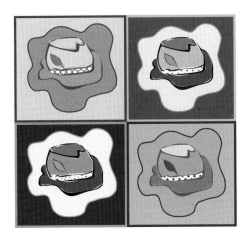

The Color and Swatches palettes let you apply, modify, and save colors in your artwork. You can paint with CMYK, RGB, HSB, and spot colors, and you also paint in shades of gray. In addition, you can paint objects with patterns and gradients.

In this lesson, you'll learn how to do the following:

- Paint with, create, and edit colors
- Name and save colors, and build a color palette
- Work with spot colors
- Copy paint attributes from one object to another
- Adjust the saturation of a color

Filling with color

Painting objects with colors, gradients, or patterns is done using a combination of palettes and tools—including the Color palette, the Swatches palette, the Gradient palette, the Stroke palette, and the paint buttons in the toolbox, which let you select and change an object's fill and line (or *stroke*) attributes.

You'll begin by filling an object with color. Filling an object paints the area enclosed by the path.

1 Choose File > Open, and locate and open the Color.ai file in the Lesson04 folder. This folder is inside the Lessons folder in the AICIB folder on your hard drive.

(To see a sample of the finished artwork, open the Color2.ai file in the Lesson04 folder, inside the Samples folder in the AICIB folder on your hard drive.)

2 Choose File > Save As, name the file Color01.ai; then click Save.

When you first open a document in Illustrator, the Color palette and Swatches palette appear by default on the right side of the window in separate groups. The Color palette displays sliders for mixing colors, and includes a color bar at the bottom.

3 If the Color and Swatches palettes aren't visible, display them by choosing Window > Show Color and Window > Show Swatches.

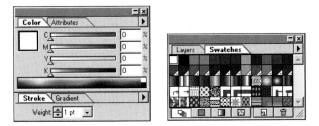

4 If the Info palette is open, close it. You won't need this palette for this lesson.

5 Click the selection tool (➤) in the toolbox, and then click the rectangular border around the artwork to select the artwork.

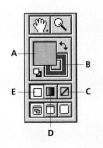

The selected object's paint attributes appear in the toolbox.

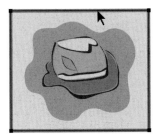

A. Fill B. Stroke C. None
D. Gradient E. Solid Color

The Fill box in the toolbox appears in the foreground, indicating that it is selected, and displays a warm gray color—the same as the fill color of the selected rectangle in the artwork. The Solid Color button is grayed, indicating that it is selected. In the background behind the Fill box, the Stroke box has a turquoise outline, indicating that the rectangle is outlined in turquoise. To change the color of an object's fill, click the Fill box to bring it forward. To change the color of an object's stroke, click the Stroke box to bring it forward.

The Color palette displays the current color as well, and its CMYK sliders show the color's percentage of cyan, magenta, yellow, and black. At the bottom of the Color palette is the color bar. Now you will use it to select a fill color of gold.

6 Position the pointer over the color bar and drag. As you drag, the color updates in the Fill boxes in the toolbox and in the Color palette.

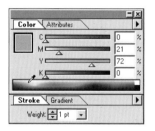

The color bar lets you quickly pick a fill or stroke color from a spectrum of colors and select colors visually. You can also choose white or black by clicking the white color box or black color box on the right end of the color bar.

7 Now, click a gold color in the color bar to select the color. The color in the Fill box in the toolbox, in the Color palette, and in the artwork is updated.

The paint attributes you choose are assigned to all new objects you create until you change the attributes again. The last paint attribute selected, either Fill or Stroke, appears selected and frontmost in the toolbox.

 Brush up on defining colors and learn how to use transparent fills in your illustrations in the "Filling shapes" lesson in Module 3 of the online companion course.

Stroking with color

Next, you'll outline the squiggly area around the hat. Painting just the outline of an object is called *stroking*.

1 Using the selection tool (↖), click the squiggly shape around the hat.

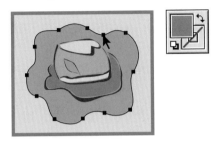

The Fill box in the toolbox displays a pale green color. The Stroke box in the background has a red slash, indicating no stroke (a stroke of "None").

You'll start by transferring the fill color to the stroke.

2 Click the Swap color button to reverse the fill and the stroke colors. The Swap color button is a quick way to reverse these colors.

The Fill box now has no fill (a fill of "None") and the Stroke box has a pale green color. (The color will become apparent in the next step.) With a fill of none, you can see through to the fill underneath—in this case, the gold color you selected in the previous procedure.

Now you'll change the weight of the line that you just stroked using the Stroke palette. *Stroke weight* is the thickness of a line. In the Stroke palette, the line has a weight of 1 point.

3 In the Stroke palette, enter 7 in the Stroke Weight text box. Press Tab, Return, or Enter to apply the change. The squiggly line now stands out.

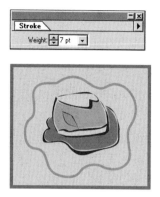

Next, you'll change the line from solid to dashed.

4 Position the pointer on the black arrow in the upper right of the Stroke palette and drag to choose Show Options from the palette menu.

You use these options to specify how to join and end lines and to make lines dashed or dotted.

5 Drag the Stroke palette by its tab so that the Color, Swatches, and Strokes palettes all are visible on-screen.

6 Select the Dashed Line option. The Dash and Gap text boxes become active.

To create a dashed or dotted line, you specify the size of the length of the dash (or dot) and then the gap, or spacing, between the dashes. You can create a dashed or dotted line with as few as two values or as many as six values. The more values you enter, the more complex the pattern.

7 Enter the following values in the Dash and Gap text boxes: 12, 0, 12, 0, 12.

Now you'll select a cap style for the dotted line.

8 In the Cap options section of the Stroke palette, click the Round Cap button (the middle button). Notice that the ends of the dashes are rounded. (Use the zoom tool to zoom in on the dashed line and view the rounded caps at the ends of the dashes if you can't see the effect in the current view.)

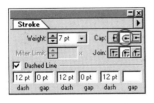

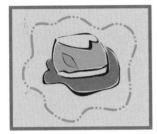

For examples of other effects you can create, see "Dashed line effects" in Chapter 9 of the *Adobe Illustrator User Guide* or in online Help. For more information about stroking lines, see "Setting line attributes" in Chapter 9 of the *Adobe Illustrator User Guide* or in online Help.

9 Click away from the artwork to deselect it.

 For more practice changing the color and thickness of outlines, take the "Stroking outlines" lesson in Module 3 of the online companion course.

Building a custom palette

Now you'll learn how to create your own custom palettes by mixing colors, saving them, and naming them in the Swatches palette.

Mixing your own color

You'll start to create a custom palette by mixing a color using the CMYK sliders in the Color palette.

1 Using the selection tool (↖), click the middle of the hat.

In the Color palette, notice that the hat color is grayscale—that is, a percentage of black—and only a K (black) slider shows a value. The color bar changes to display a scale ramp from white to black.

Now you'll change the color model to CMYK so that you can mix colors.

2 In the Color palette, select the black triangle in the upper right corner, and drag to display the Color palette menu.

3 From the Color palette menu, choose CMYK.

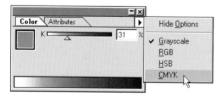

The Color palette lets you edit and mix colors—either colors that you create or colors that you have selected from the Swatches palette, from an object, or from a color library. In this case, you're choosing colors using the CMYK color model.

Commonly used for printing inks, the CMYK color model lets you choose a color with cyan, magenta, yellow and black values ranging from 0 to 100%. You can also choose from the following models:

• RGB, which lets you choose a color with red, green, and blue values ranging from 0 to 255. The RGB color model commonly is used for the Web and other on-screen displays.

• Grayscale, which lets you specify a percentage of black from 0 to 100%.

• HSB, which lets you choose a color with a hue from 0 to 360° and with saturation and brightness values from 0 to 100%.

Now you'll select a gold color for the middle of the hat.

4 In the Color palette, drag the CMYK sliders to select a new color or enter values and press Tab, Return, or Enter. (We chose 35% magenta and 75% yellow for a gold-orange.)

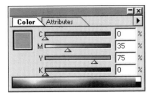

You can choose different color models and then use the Color palette sliders to select a color precisely by its color values.

5 Click away from the artwork to deselect it.

Saving colors

You'll add the gold color you just mixed to the Swatches palette.

The Swatches palette stores the colors, gradients, and patterns that have been pre-loaded into Adobe Illustrator as well as those you have created and saved for reuse. Opening a new artwork file displays the default set of swatches that comes with the Adobe Illustrator program.

1 Drag the Resize box (Macintosh) at the bottom of the Swatches palette or click the Maximize button (Windows) to enlarge the palette.

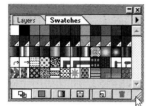

You can select a color to add from either the Fill or Stroke box in the toolbox, or from the Color palette. Even though you deselected the artwork, the gold-orange color is still the current color in the Fill box in the toolbox and in the Color palette.

2 Drag the swatch from the Fill box in the toolbox to an empty spot in the Swatches palette.

As you drag the color into the Swatches palette, an outline appears around the palette, indicating that it is active and that you are about to drop the color.

Colors stored in the Swatches palette are saved with the current document. Each new Adobe Illustrator document can have a different set of swatches stored in its Swatches palette.

Now you'll add another color to the Swatches palette.

3 Using the selection tool (▸), select the rectangular border around the entire artwork.

4 Click the New Swatch button at the bottom of the Swatches palette to store the color.

You can drag and drop colors into the Swatches palette, or you can click the New Swatch button to store colors.

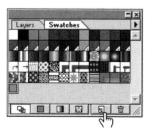

You can also make your own custom set of swatches and delete swatches from the Swatches palette that you don't use.

5 To delete a swatch, click it in the Swatches palette; to select multiple swatches, Shift-click the swatches. Then click the Trash button at the bottom of the Swatches palette, and click OK at the prompt to delete the colors.

The deletion affects only the current document's palette. Any objects already painted with a deleted color aren't affected. If you want to add a color back into the Swatches palette, you can drag the color directly from the Color palette or from the Fill or Stroke box in the toolbox. You can also restore the default set of colors to your artwork. New documents always begin with the same default palette.

6 To retrieve the default set of swatches, choose Window > Swatch Libraries > Default.

You can also choose to display the Macintosh system palette, the Windows system palette, or the Web palette using the Swatch Libraries command.

Naming a color

You can also store colors by name and then paint objects in your artwork by color name for consistency.

All colors—both process colors and spot colors—can be named while still retaining all characteristics of the color mode (for example, CMYK, RGB, HSB, or Grayscale mode).

1 Double-click the gold swatch you just saved in the Swatches palette, or choose Swatch Options from the Swatches palette menu.

2 In the Swatch Options dialog box, name the color (for example, "hat-gold").

The Swatches palette and the Swatches dialog boxes let you name, store, and select colors in one of two modes: as colors that are printed as process colors (these include CMYK, RGB, and HSB colors, and grayscale), and as *spot colors*. Spot colors are special premixed colors, including those from color matching libraries such as PANTONE®. Spot colors are used instead of, or in addition to, process color inks, and require their own separations and their own plates on press.

Note: You can also use spot colors while designing artwork on your screen, and then have them converted to process colors when you print your artwork.

3 Click OK.

Now you'll change the display of the Swatches palette so that you can locate the color by name.

4 Choose Name from the Swatches palette menu to display the swatches by name.

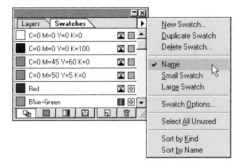

5 Scroll to the bottom of the list in the Swatches palette to see the swatch you just named.

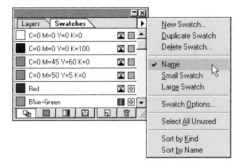

A. CMYK B. Spot Color C. RGB

You can change how swatches are displayed in the palette—as large or small swatches, or by name. When you display swatches by name, the Swatches palette also displays icons indicating whether the color is RGB, CMYK, or spot.

Using a color matching system

Next, you will paint with a predefined spot color from another color matching system.

You'll start by opening a color library.

1 Choose Window > Swatch Libraries > PANTONE® Coated.

The Swatch Libraries command lets you select from a range of color libraries—including the PANTONE® Coated, Toyo Ink Electronic Color Finder 1050, the FOCOLTONE® COLOUR SYSTEM, and the TRUMATCH™ system. Each color system that you select appears as a separate Swatch Library palette, identified by its tab. When you import color libraries into Adobe Illustrator, the colors in the library are locked: They cannot be deleted, modified, or edited. You can, however, add the colors to the Swatches palette to modify them or to build your own custom set of colors.

2 Using the selection tool (▶), click the feather to select it.

3 In the PANTONE palette, scroll to PANTONE 185 CVC in the list.

To use the PANTONE printing ink colors, you should first determine the ink color you want by using a PANTONE book such as the *PANTONE Color Formula Guide 747XR* or an ink chart obtained from your printer. PANTONE books are available from print shops and graphic arts supply houses.

In the PANTONE palette menu on the right side, notice the square icon with a dot in the center. This button indicates that the color is a spot color.

4 Click to select the color and paint the feather.

5 In the Color palette, drag the Tint slider to adjust the tint of the spot color.

Next, you'll add the color to the Swatches palette. To modify or edit a color from an imported library (for example, to convert it to its CMYK color equivalents), you must first copy the color in the color library to the Swatches palette.

6 From the PANTONE palette menu, choose Add to Swatches.

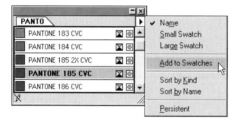

You can also drag the PANTONE color from either the Fill box in the toolbox or from the box in the Color palette to the Swatches palette, or click the New Swatch button at the bottom of the Swatches palette to add the color.

Now you'll convert the spot color to a process color.

7 In the Swatches palette, double-click the color to display the Swatch Options dialog box. You can also choose Swatch Options from the Swatches palette menu.

8 Name the color. From the Color Mode menu, choose Process Color. Name the color (such as "scarlet feather") and click OK.

In the Swatches palette, a solid square next to the swatch name indicates that the color is now a process color. (If you're viewing the Swatches palette by small or large swatches, a white triangle in the corner of a swatch indicates a spot color.)

Notice that the Color palette now displays the CMYK values of the color.

Converting a spot color to a process color changes the type of color you're working with, and lets you edit the individual color components. (Adobe Illustrator converts spot colors to process colors for printing, unless you deselect the Convert to Process option in the Separation Setup dialog box. For more information on making and printing separations, see Lesson 21, "Printing Artwork and Producing Color Separations.")

9 Deselect the artwork.

10 Close the PANTONE library.

Copying paint attributes

You can use the eyedropper tool to copy colors from your artwork into the Color palette. Also called *sampling*, copying colors lets you replicate paint attributes even when you don't know their exact values.

1 Select the eyedropper tool (✐) in the toolbox.

2 Click the brim of the hat. This action picks up the paint attributes of the hat brim and displays them in the Color palette.

Clicking with the eyedropper tool also applies the sampled paint attributes to any selected object in the artwork.

By default, the eyedropper and paint bucket tools affect all paint attributes of an object. However, you can restrict what attributes are affected. For more information, see "Copying and applying paint attributes with the eyedropper and paint bucket tools" in Chapter 10 of the *Adobe Illustrator User Guide* and in online Help.

3 To quickly apply the current paint attributes to the crown of the hat, hold down Option (Macintosh) or Alt (Windows) to select the paint bucket tool (✋), and click the crown of the hat. This action also selects the crown of the hat.

When the paint bucket or eyedropper tool is selected, you can hold down Option (Macintosh) or Alt (Windows) to select the other tool.

You can also drag a color from the Swatches palette and drop it onto an object to change its color without selecting the object.

Desaturating colors

Next, you'll desaturate part of the hat artwork.

1 Select the crown of the hat, if it is not already selected.

2 Make sure that the Fill box is selected in the toolbox.

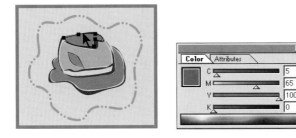

3 In the Color palette, hold down Command+Shift (Macintosh) or Alt+Shift (Windows), and drag one of the CMYK sliders that has a value. (If you drag a slider that is set to 0, you will select a new color.)

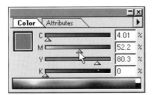

As you drag, the sliders move in tandem, and the intensity of the color is adjusted. Adjusting the saturation of a color lets you change its strength without affecting the color (hue).

Another way to adjust the saturation of colors is by using the Saturate filter. This filter saturates or desaturates the colors of selected objects by increasing or decreasing the percentages of color values. Thus you can adjust the values of multiple colors at once.

You'll try out the Saturate filter on the artwork.

4 Choose Edit > Select all to select all of the artwork.

5 Choose Filter > Colors > Saturate.

6 Select the Preview option to help gauge the effect. Then drag the Intensity slider to increase and decrease the strength of the color throughout the artwork.

Notice that as the value increases, the colors become very rich; as the value decreases, the colors appear washed out.

7 Increase the intensity and the saturation to 25%. Click OK.

Filling with a pattern

Now you'll fill the hat ribbon with a pattern. You select patterns using the Swatches palette.

1 Using the selection tool (✸), click the hat ribbon.

The Fill box in the toolbox shows that the hat ribbon's current fill is gray.

From the Swatches palette menu, choose Small Swatch to display the palette as swatches.

The buttons at the bottom of the Swatches palette let you display swatches grouped as solid colors, gradients, or patterns.

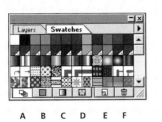

A. *Show All Swatches* B. *Show Color Swatches* C. *Show Gradient Swatches* D. *Show Pattern Swatches* E. *New Swatch* F. *Delete Swatch*

2 Click the Pattern button, the fourth button from the left. A palette of patterns appears.

3 Click a pattern in the palette to select it and fill the hat ribbon.

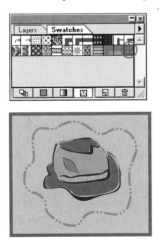

Learn how to control the stacking order of shapes and improve the look of your artwork. Take the "Stacking objects" lesson in Module 3 of the online companion course.

Changing paint attributes throughout your artwork

As a final step, you'll select several different objects with the same fill color and globally adjust the fill. You'll use one of the Select commands to quickly select all of the outlines.

1 Select the outline of the hat.

2 Choose Edit > Select > Same Fill Color.

You can also select multiple objects in your artwork by the same stroke color, stroke weight, or paint attributes. The Select commands are handy for making global changes to your artwork.

3 Select another fill color for the hat outlines using one of the techniques that you learned in this lesson—by dragging in the color bar, dragging the Color palette sliders, or clicking a swatch in the Swatches palette.

4 Choose File > Close to close the Color01.ai file. If desired, save your changes.

You've completed painting the hat artwork using a variety of painting tools.

For information about painting with spot colors, patterns, and gradient fills, see "Painting" (Chapter 9) in the *Adobe Illustrator User Guide* or in online Help.

Now that you've mastered a variety of shape and painting tools, apply what you've learned in the student project in Module 3 of the online companion course.

Review

• Describe two ways to fill an object.

(1) You select the object, click the Fill box in the toolbox to select the option, and then display the Color palette. You can use the Color palette, color bar, or Swatches palette to select a color, gradient, or pattern. (2) You can also use the eyedropper tool to sample the paint attributes of one object and paste them onto another object.

• How can you determine the current paint settings of an object?

You select the object, and click the Fill box or Stroke box in the toolbox, and then look at the current attributes in the Color palette.

• Name two different color models.

Adobe Illustrator lets you choose from four different color models. (1) The CMYK color model lets you mix a color with cyan, magenta, yellow and black values ranging from 0 to 100%. (2) The RGB color model lets you choose a color with red, green, and blue values ranging from 0 to 255. (3) The Grayscale color model lets you apply a percentage of black from 0 to 100%.(4) The HSB color model lets you mix a color with a hue from 0 to 360º and with saturation and brightness values from 0 to 100%.

• How do you control the line attributes of a stroked object?

You use the Stroke palette to select the line weight, solid or dashed attributes, end caps, joins, and other attributes for lines.

• How do you store a color in your artwork?

You use the Swatches palette to store a color. You drag the selected color to the Swatches palette from the Color palette or from the Fill or Stroke boxes in the toolbox.

• What happens when you delete a swatch from your artwork?

The action cannot be undone. Only your current document's palette is affected when you delete a swatch. An object in the artwork painted with the swatch color is unaffected. New documents always begin with the same default palette.

• What is a spot color? What is a process color?

A process color is a grayscale, or a CMYK, RGB, or HSB color. A spot color is a special premixed color, including from a color matching library, which is used instead of, or in addition to, process color inks, and requires its own separation and its own plate on press.

Lesson 5

Lesson 5

Drawing Straight Lines

You draw straight lines by using the pen tool to create a starting anchor point and an ending anchor point. In this lesson, you will draw elements of the plant illustration using straight line segments. You will also edit the segments to modify some of the shapes.

In this lesson, you'll learn how to do the following:

- Draw straight lines
- End segments
- Constrain drawing to straight lines or diagonal lines at 45° angles
- Split a path
- Add anchor points to a path

Opening a template

To begin the lesson, you'll open a template that contains several predefined views.

1 Choose File > Open, and locate and open the Pen.ai file in the Lesson5 folder. This folder is inside the Lessons folder in the AICIB folder on your hard drive.)

(To see a sample of the finished artwork, open the Pen2.ai file in Lesson05, inside the Samples folder in the AICIB folder on your hard drive.)

2 Choose File > Save As, name the file Pen01.ai, and click Save.

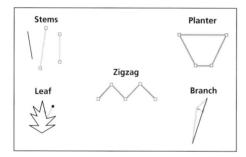

The Pen.ai document is a template that contains all the elements of the plant drawing and several custom views. Custom views are scrolling and magnification settings you can name and save with a document. (For more information on custom views, see "Creating custom views" in Chapter 3 of the *Adobe Illustrator User Guide* or in online Help.)

3 Choose View > View Stems to select a magnified view of the straight lines representing the stems of the plant.

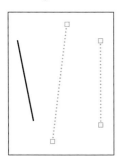

The first line has already been drawn.

4 Click the selection tool (⬧), and then click the line to select it. The line consists of a straight line segment connected by two anchor points.

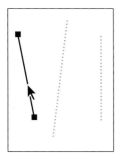

Notice that the paint attributes of the selected line (a black stroke and no fill) appear in the toolbox. (For more on paint attributes, see Lesson 4, "Painting" or see "Painting" (Chapter 9) in the *Adobe Illustrator User Guide*, or in online Help.)

Drawing straight lines

To draw straight lines with the pen tool, you click to create a starting anchor point and click to set an ending anchor point.

1 Select the pen tool (✎).

2 Move the pen tool pointer to the middle line on the template.

Notice that the pen tool pointer has a small *x* next to it. This indicates that clicking will begin a new path.

3 Follow instruction A on the template. When you clicked the mouse button, you created an anchor point—a small solid square.

4 Follow instruction B on the template to draw the second line.

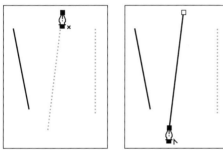

Click once to begin a straight line.   *Click again to end it.*

When you click a second time, a carat appears over the last selected anchor point next to the pen tool. This carat indicates that if you click again, you will split the anchor point and create a direction line that can be manipulated. The carat disappears when you move the pen tool away from the anchor point.

You must end the path before you can draw new segments that aren't added to the path.

5 End the path using one of the following methods:

• Hold down Command (Macintosh) or Ctrl (Windows) to activate the current selection tool, and click away from the path to deselect it.

• Choose Edit > Deselect All.

Keeping lines vertical, horizontal, and diagonal

You can draw lines that are vertical, horizontal, or diagonal by holding down Shift. This is called *constraining* the line.

1 Following instructions C and D on the template, hold down Shift as you use the pen tool to draw the third line.

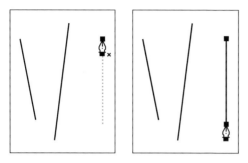

Holding down Shift as you click constrains the tool to the nearest 45° angle from the Constrain Angle setting in the General Preferences dialog box. (The Constrain Angle is set to 0° by default. To change it, choose File > Preferences > General.)

2 Deselect the line by holding down Command (Macintosh) or Ctrl (Windows) and clicking away from the line

Next, you'll draw zigzag lines and constrain them diagonally.

3 To display an enlarged view of the zigzag line on the template, choose View > View Zigzag.

4 Using the pen tool, follow instructions A through E to create a symmetrical zigzag line.

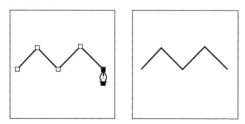

You can draw a line that has as many connected points as you want.

5 Deselect the line by Command-clicking (Macintosh) or Ctrl-clicking (Windows) away from the line.

In drawing these straight lines, you have drawn *open paths*—paths that have a distinct beginning and end. You can also draw *closed paths*—paths that loop and have no end point.

Closing paths

Now you will draw a closed shape.

1 To display an enlarged view of the planter on the template, choose View > View Planter.

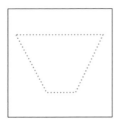

2 Using the pen tool, follow instructions A through E on the template.

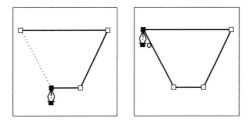

Note that an open circle appears next to the pen tool when you position it exactly over the starting anchor point, indicating that clicking will close the path. The next time you click with the pen tool, you'll begin a new path rather than continuing this one.

 Explore the power of the pen tool by taking the "Pencil vs. pen" lesson in Module 4 of the online companion course.

Splitting a path

Next, you will split an existing path using the scissors tool and adjust the shape of the path.

1 To display an enlarged view of the leaf shape on the template, choose View > View Leaf.

2 Select the scissors tool (✂) in the toolbox.

3 Follow instructions A through D to split the long line segment and to use the direct-selection tool (k) to adjust its lower half.

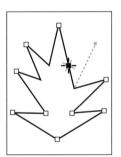

Click with the scissors tool to cut a line.

Drag to separate the new line segments.

Cuts made with the scissors tool must be on a line or a curve rather than on an endpoint.

Note: *You can select the direct-selection tool from the keyboard without deselecting the scissors tool. Press Command+Tab (Macintosh) or Ctrl+Tab (Windows) to switch to the direct-selection tool; then press Command/Ctrl to use it.*

Where you click, you see a new selected anchor point. However, the scissors tool actually creates two anchor points each time you click. Because they are on top of each other, you can see only one.

4 Now select the pen tool ( ).

5 Follow instruction E on the template.

Note that a slash appears next to the pen tool when you position it exactly over the anchor point.

6 Follow instruction F on the template to add a segment and close the shape.

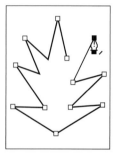
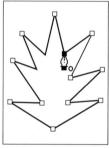

Clicking pen tool with slash draws path from anchor point.

Circle indicates path will be closed.

When you position the pen tool over the anchor point you dragged to the green dot, a slash appears next to the pen tool. The slash indicates that clicking the pen tool on this unselected anchor point will let you draw from that point.

When you close the path in instruction F, the open circle appears next to the pen tool.

Adding anchor points

To complete the lesson, you will add an anchor point to an existing path using the add-anchor-point tool, and then modify the shape of the path. Adding anchor points can give you more control over the path shape.

1 To display an enlarged view of the straight line representing a branch of the plant, choose View > View Branch.

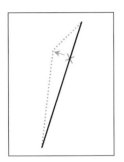

2 Position the pointer on the pen tool (✒) in the toolbox, and drag to the right to select the add-anchor-point tool (✒₊)

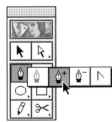

3 Follow instructions A and B.

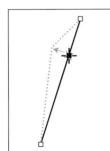 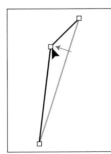

Click to add an anchor point.

Drag new anchor point with direct-selection tool.

You can switch to the direct-selection tool from the keyboard by pressing Command (Macintosh) or Ctrl (Windows).

You can also add anchor points to a path using the Object > Path > Add Anchor Points command. This command adds an anchor point between a pair of anchor points.

For more information on how to add and delete anchor points, see "Adding and deleting anchor points" in Chapter 5 of the *Adobe Illustrator User Guide* or in online Help.

Using a context-sensitive menu

Now you'll use a context-sensitive menu to practice choosing some commands and return the line to its original condition.

In addition to the menus that appear at the top of your screen, Adobe Illustrator contains a number of context-sensitive menus. These menus display commands that relate to the active tool, selection, or palette.

1 Position the pointer over the path that you just adjusted.

2 On the Macintosh, press Control and hold down the mouse button. In Windows, right-click the mouse button to display the context-sensitive menu. (On the Macintosh, you must continue to hold down Control to see the context-sensitive menu.)

3 From the menu, choose Undo Move and then choose Undo Add Anchor. (The pointer must be on the path when you press Control or right-click the mouse button to display the relevant context menu.)

4 Then use the context-sensitive menu to redo instructions A and B on the template.

Notice that the context-sensitive menu has a Redo command.

5 Choose File > Close, and if desired, save any changes to the Pen01.ai file.

This completes the line drawing lesson. For more practice with the pen tool, go on to Lesson 6, "Drawing Curves."

For more information about the pen tool, see the "Drawing and Selecting" movie on the Adobe Illustrator Tour and Training CD; or see "Drawing with the pen tool" in Chapter 5 of the *Adobe Illustrator User Guide* or in online Help.

Review

• How do you draw a horizontal or vertical line with the pen tool?

You click with the pen tool to draw straight lines, and you hold down the Shift key as you click with the pen tool to draw horizontal or vertical lines.

• Describe one way to end a path.

To end a path you can hold down Command (Macintosh) or Ctrl (Windows) to activate the current selection tool, and click away from the path to deselect it. You can also choose Edit > Deselect All.

• What happens if you don't end a path?

If you don't end a path, any new segments you draw with the pen tool will be added to the path.

• How do you add anchor points to a path? When might it be useful to add anchor points?

You can add anchor points using the add-anchor-point tool or the Object > Path > Add Anchor Points command. Added anchor points let you edit a segment; for example, you could add anchor points to a straight line and then move the segments to create a zigzag or wavy line.

• How do you split a path? What is created when you split a path?

To split a path, click with the scissors tool on a segment or curve. The scissors tool creates two anchor points, one on top of the other.

• What is a context-sensitive menu? How do you display one?

A context-sensitive menu displays commands that relate to the active tool, selection, or palette. To display a menu, press Control and hold down the mouse button (Macintosh) or right-click the mouse button (Windows).

Lesson 6

Lesson 6

Drawing Curves

In addition to drawing straight lines, the pen tool lets you draw precise curves and complex shapes. You'll practice drawing with the pen tool by creating an illustration of a pear.

In this lesson, you'll learn how to do the following:

• Draw curves

• Select curve segments and adjust them

• Draw different types of curves, smooth and pointed

• Change a curve to a point and a point to a curve

Drawing curves

In this part of the lesson, you'll learn how to draw smooth curved lines with the pen tool. In vector drawing programs such as Adobe Illustrator, you draw a curve, called a Bézier curve, by setting anchor points and dragging to define the shape of the curve. Although this takes some getting used to, this type of drawing gives you the most control and flexibility in computer graphics.

You'll begin by drawing a single curve and then draw a series of curves together, using a file containing some guidelines to help you.

1 Choose File > Open, and locate and open the Curves.ai file in the Lesson06 folder. This folder is inside the Lessons folder in the AICIB folder on your hard drive.

(To see a sample of the finished artwork, open the Curves2.ai file in the Lesson06 folder, inside the Samples folder in the AICIB folder on your hard drive.)

2 Choose File > Save As, name the file Curves01.ai; then click Save.

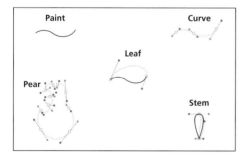

A template containing various parts of a pear appears. You will use the template to practice drawing and editing curves with the pen tool.

Like the Pen.ai document in the previous lesson, the Curves.ai document includes several preset views.

3 Choose View > View Paint to display an enlarged view of a curve on the template.

4 Click the direct-selection tool (⌖) in the toolbox. This selection tool lets you select and edit individual curve segments.

5 Click the curve to view its anchor points and its direction lines, which extend from the points.

As their names imply, the anchor points anchor the curved segments, and the direction lines control the direction of the curves. By selecting the curve, you also select the paint attributes of the curve so that the next line you draw will have the same attributes. (For more on paint attributes, see the Lesson 4, "Painting"; or see "Painting" [Chapter 9] of the *Adobe Illustrator User Guide*, or online Help.)

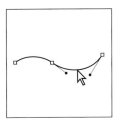

6 Now choose View > View Curve to display an enlarged view of the first curve you'll draw.

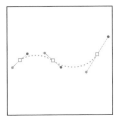

To draw a curve, you set an anchor point and drag to determine the curve's direction. By pressing the mouse button, you set an anchor point; as you drag from the anchor point, direction lines form.

7 Select the pen tool (✒). Follow instruction A on the template to set the starting anchor point and direction lines of the curve.

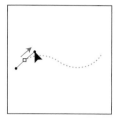

Next, you'll set the second anchor point and its direction lines.

8 Follow instruction B on the template. Illustrator connects the two anchor points with a curve that follows the direction lines you have created.

Notice that if you vary the angle of dragging, you change the amount of curve. If you make a mistake, choose Edit > Undo.

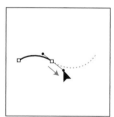

You can drag the direction lines or their endpoints, called *direction points*, to adjust the shape of the curve. Anchor points, direction points, and direction lines are aids to help you draw. They always appear in the current selection color—in this case, light blue.

Anchor points are square, and when selected appear filled; unselected, they appear unfilled, like hollow squares. Direction points are round. These lines and points do not print with the artwork.

9 Now follow instruction C on the template to finish drawing the curve.

You always must indicate when you have finished drawing a path. You do this by clicking the pen tool in the toolbox, by Command-clicking (Macintosh) or Ctrl-clicking (Windows) away from the artwork, or by choosing Edit > Deselect All.

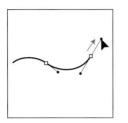

10 Command-click (Macintosh) or Ctrl-click (Windows) away from the artwork to deselect it.

Drawing different kinds of curves

Now you will add to an existing curved segment. Even if you end a curve, you can return to the curve and add to it at a later time. The Option (Macintosh) or Alt (Windows) key lets you control the type of curve you draw.

1 Choose View > View Leaf to display an enlarged view of a partially completed leaf.

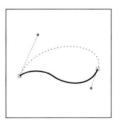

Now you will add to the path by holding down Option (Macintosh) or Alt (Windows), and dragging with the pen tool to create a *corner point*. A corner point lets you change the direction of the curve. A smooth point lets you draw a continuous curve.

2 Follow instruction A on the template.

Note that as you hold down Option/Alt over the anchor point, the status line in the lower left corner of the window displays: "Pen: Make Corner."

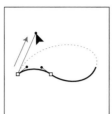

Slash indicates pen tool is aligned with anchor.

Option/Alt-dragging creates corner point.

So far, all of the paths you have drawn in this lesson have been open paths. Now you'll draw a closed path, in which the final anchor point is drawn on the first anchor point of the path. (Examples of closed paths include ovals and rectangles.) You'll close the path using a smooth point.

3 Follow instruction B on the template.

Notice the direction lines where you close the path. The direction lines on both sides of a smooth point are aligned along the same angle.

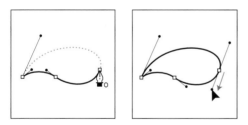

4 Choose View > View Pear to display an enlarged view of the pear.

Now you'll draw a single, continuous object that contains smooth points and corner points. Each time you want to change the direction of a curve at a point, you'll hold down Option (Macintosh) or Alt (Windows) to create a corner point.

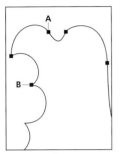

A. *Smooth point*
B. *Corner point*

5 Follow instructions A through D on the template to draw the bite marks in the pear. If you cannot see all of the outline on your screen, use the scroll bars to bring it into view.

At points B, C, and D, you first drag to continue the current segment, and then Option/Alt-drag to set the direction of the next curved segment.

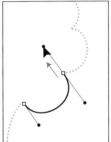
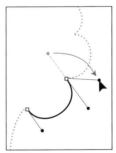

Dragging adjusts curve.

Option/Alt-dragging direction point sets corner point.

Next, you'll continue drawing the pear by creating smooth points with the pen tool.

6 Follow instructions E through K to complete and close the pear shape.

7 Hold down Command (Macintosh) or Ctrl (Windows), and click away from the path to deselect it.

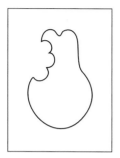

Q *Sometimes it's tricky to make curved segments meet at a corner. Get some inside tips on ways to make this easy in the "Mixing corners and curves" lesson in Module 4 of the online companion course.*

Editing curves

To adjust the curves you've drawn, you can drag the curve's anchor points or its direction lines.

You can also edit a curve by moving the line.

1 Select the direct-selection tool (↖). You use this tool to adjust a segment of a curve.

2 Click the outline of the pear.

Clicking with the direct-selection tool displays the curve's direction lines and lets you adjust the shape of individual curved segments. Clicking with the selection tool selects the entire path.

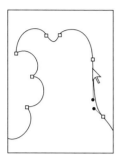

Using direct-selection tool
selects curved segment.

(For more information on the selection tools, see Lesson 2, "Making Selections"; see the movie "Drawing and Selecting" on the Adobe Illustrator Tour and Training CD; or see "Selecting objects" in Chapter 5 of the *Adobe Illustrator User Guide* or in online Help.)

3 Click the anchor point at the top right of the pear, and adjust the segment by dragging the top direction point as shown in the illustration.

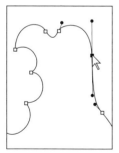 

Selecting anchor point   Adjusting direction point

Tips for drawing curves

As you continue to practice drawing curves, you may find these guidelines helpful:

• Drag in the direction of the bump of the curve you are about to create. For an upward curve, drag the first point up. For a downward curve, drag the first point down.

• To control the shape and size of the curve, drag a direction point about a third of the curve's total length if it were stretched out flat. The angle in which you drag also affects the curve's shape and size. Remember, however, that you can always adjust a curve after you've drawn it.

• Try to put anchor points at the sides of the curve rather than on the top of the bump. Placed on the sides, anchor points are easier to edit to control the curve.

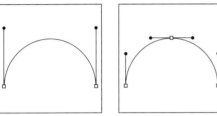

More efficient curve   *Less efficient curve*

• Use as few anchor points as you can to fit the curve. Think of taking big, broad steps when you draw curves. Again, you can always adjust the curve after you've drawn it.

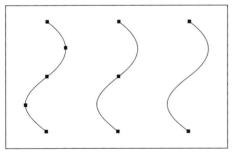

Least to most efficient curves, from left to right

An efficient curve uses the least number of anchor points needed to create the curve, and thus prints and displays faster.

Changing a smooth curve to a corner point and vice versa

To complete this lesson, you'll adjust a curve by converting a smooth point to a corner point, and a corner point to a smooth point.

1 Choose View > View Stem to display an enlarged view of the stem.

2 Click the direct-selection tool (▸) in the toolbox, and follow instruction A on the template to display the direction lines for the top smooth point.

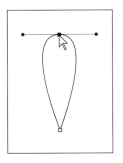

3 Do one of the following to select the convert-direction-point tool (⅄):

• Select the pen tool in the toolbox, and drag to the right to select the convert-direction-point tool.

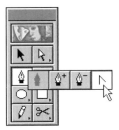

• When the direct-selection tool is the current tool, press Command+Option (Macintosh) or Ctrl+Alt (Windows) to get the convert-direction-point tool.

When the pen tool is the current tool, press Option (Macintosh) or Alt (Windows) to use the shortcut to get the convert-direction point tool.

4 Follow instruction B on the template to adjust the curve's left side.

Dragging the direction point with the convert-direction-point tool "breaks" the direction line (changes its angle) and converts the anchor point to a corner point.

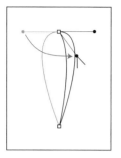

5 Using the convert-direction-point tool, follow instruction C on the template to convert the bottom corner point to a smooth point, rounding out the curve.

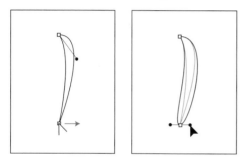

6 Position the convert-direction-point tool over the bottom anchor point, and drag to the red dot. Two direction lines emerge from the anchor point, indicating that it is now a smooth point.

The convert-direction-point tool lets you adjust just one of the curve's direction lines, creating a corner point. Where you drag with the convert-direction-point tool determines whether you create a smooth point or a corner point. Keep these guidelines in mind:

• Drag from the curve's anchor point for a smooth point and continuous curve.

• Drag a handle (direction point) of the curve for a discontinuous curve with a corner point.

7 Choose File > Close, save your changes if desired, and close the file.

You've completed the drawing curves lesson. For additional practice with the pen tool, try tracing over images with it. As you practice more with the pen tool, you'll become more adept at drawing the kinds of curves and shapes you want.

For more information on the pen tool, see the movie "Drawing and Selecting" on the Adobe Illustrator Tour and Training CD-ROM; or see "Drawing with the pen tool" in Chapter 5 of the *Adobe Illustrator User Guide* or in online Help.

Sometimes you just can't avoid reshaping paths. For special tips on how to do this, take the "Reshaping a path" lesson in Module 4 of the online companion course.

Review

• How do you draw a smooth curve?

You drag with the pen tool, once in the direction of the curve's bump, and a second time in the opposite direction.

• How do you control the shape of a curve?

You drag the direction lines in the direction you want the curve to follow.

• How do you make a curve with a sharp change in a direction (a corner point)?

Press Option (Macintosh) or Alt (Windows), and click on a direction point to "break" the direction line.

• What are direction lines and points? What purpose do they serve?

Direction lines emerge from anchor points; both are aids to control the shape of your curve. Direction lines control the direction of the curve; their endpoints are called direction points. You drag these points to adjust a curve.

• How do you edit a curve's direction lines?

You use the direct-selection tool (▸) to select the curve's direction lines and edit them by dragging.

• What tool do you use to convert a smooth point to a corner point? To convert a corner point to a smooth point?

You use the convert-direction-point tool (⊾) for both purposes. To convert a smooth point to a corner point, drag from a direction point with the convert-direction-point tool. To convert a corner point to a smooth point, use the tool to drag from an anchor point with the convert-direction-point tool.

• What does a slash next to the pen tool indicate?

A slash indicates that the pen tool is aligned with the anchor point.

• What makes a curve efficient?

The fewer the anchor points on a curve, the more efficient the curve. An efficient curve uses the least number of anchor points needed to create the curve, and thus prints and displays faster.

• What is the difference between an open path and a closed path?

An open path has distinct end points, and can be continued from one of them. A closed path has the final anchor point drawn on the first anchor point of the path and has no obvious beginning or end.

Lesson 7

Lesson 7
Tracing Over a Placed Image

It's often helpful to use a photograph or pencil sketch as a reference for creating a detailed drawing in Illustrator. You can place an image in an Illustrator document, and then use it as a template for tracing outlines and fine details with any of the drawing tools.

In this lesson, you'll learn to

- Place an image
- Create a new layer and set layer options
- Trace a drawing
- Change the view of a layer to Artwork or to Preview view

Placing an image

One way to trace artwork and create a new drawing is to begin by placing an image in an Illustrator document, positioning it on a layer, and dimming the layer. Illustrator can import and export many common graphic file formats, including GIF, JPEG, PICT, TIFF, PDF, and PostScript®.

1 Choose File > New to open a new file.

2 Choose File > Place.

By default, the Place command creates a link to a separate, external file. (The linked file always must accompany the Illustrator file.) A placed file that is embedded is included in the Illustrator file, resulting in a larger Illustrator file.

You can also choose to embed the file by deselecting the Link option in the Place dialog box when you place the file. Embedding a file results in a larger Illustrator file.

Placed vector artwork is converted to Illustrator paths; placed bitmap images can be modified using transformation tools and image filters.

1 Select the Fish.eps file in the Lesson07 folder. This folder is located in the Lessons folder within the AICIB folder on your hard drive.

(To see a sample of the finished artwork, open the Fish2.ai file in the Lesson07 folder in the Samples folder within the AICIB folder on your hard drive.)

2 Deselect the Link option. Then click Place.

This image was created by retouching a scanned photograph in Adobe Photoshop.

3 Using the scale tool (⬚), drag the bounding box to adjust the size of the artwork. If you don't like the adjustment, choose Edit > Undo.

You can position a placed image anywhere on the page, and you can apply transformation attributes such as scaling, rotating, reflecting, and shearing. (For more information about placed files, see "Opening and placing artwork" in Chapter 14 of the *Adobe Illustrator User Guide* or in online Help.)

Creating a tracing layer

Now you will use the Layers palette to create a layer that will act as a template over which you can trace.

1 Choose Window > Show Layers to display the Layers palette if it is not visible on-screen. The Layers palette is grouped with the Swatches palette.

2 In the Layers palette, double-click Layer 1 to display the Layer Options dialog box.

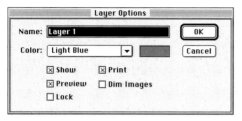

You can also choose Options for Layer 1 from the Layers palette menu to display the dialog box.

3 In the Layers Options dialog box, name the layer "Template."

Now you'll lock the layer so that it cannot be selected or edited.

4 Select the Lock option.

Next, you'll dim the layer so that any tracing over it will be more visible.

5 Select the Dim Images option.

The Dim Images option makes placed images on a given layer appear dimmed on-screen. This option screens back the placed image to make it easier to edit objects on top of the placed image. Besides its use for tracing, this option also is useful for laying out artwork on top of a placed image.

Next, you'll protect the layer from printing with the artwork.

6 Deselect the Print option.

You can deselect this option to print only the layers of your artwork that you need to proof.

7 Click OK.

In the Layers palette, notice the pencil with a slash through it, indicating that the layer is locked. You can also lock a layer after you've created it by positioning the pointer to the left of the layer name, in the blank column next to the eye icon, and clicking. Note that hiding a layer also prevents it from being edited.

Now you'll create a drawing layer.

8 In the Layers palette, click the New Layer button at the bottom of the Layers palette.

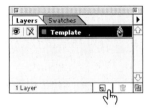

You can also choose New Layer from the Layers palette menu to create a new layer.

9 In the Layers palette, double-click the layer name to display the Layer Options dialog box.

10 Name the layer "Drawing." Deselect the Preview option, and click OK.

Deselecting the Preview option puts the layer in Artwork view (indicated by a hollow eye icon in the Layers palette), which displays objects as outlines only, with no fill or stroke colors. In Artwork view, you can draw objects over the Template layer without obscuring the artwork on the layer. In Preview view, you see the artwork as it will print.

 Put your creativity to work by importing a sketch to use as a template. Take the "Setting up a template" lesson, in Module 4 of the online companion course.

Tracing a shape

Next, you'll use a drawing tool to trace the outline of the fish. When tracing more complex shapes, use either the pen tool or pencil tool for best results. You can also use a dedicated tracing program such as Adobe Streamline™.

For tracing simpler shapes or outlines, you can also use the autotrace tool to trace the shapes or outlines automatically. The autotrace tool can trace black-and-white or color images. For more information on the tool, see "Tracing artwork" in Chapter 5 of the *Adobe Illustrator User Guide* or in online Help.

1 Select the pen tool (✒) or the pencil tool (✐), and trace the outline of the fish.

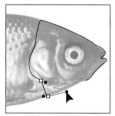

Tracing fish outline with pen tool

(See Lesson 5, "Drawing Straight Lines," and Lesson 6, "Drawing Curves" for lessons on drawing with the pen tool, and see "Drawing with the pencil tool" in Chapter 5 of the *Adobe Illustrator User Guide,* or online Help for more information on the pencil tool.)

Notice that you can trace over the locked layers without selecting or modifying the fish image.

Next, you'll switch the Drawing layer to Preview view, so that you can see the artwork as it will print.

2 Hold down Command (Macintosh) or Control (Windows), and click the eye icon next to the layer in the Layers palette.

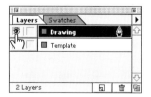

The solid eye indicates that the layer is in Preview view.

Now you'll use the Swatches palette to paint what you just traced.

3 Make sure that the fish outline you just drew is selected.

4 If the Swatches palette is not visible on-screen, choose Window > Show Swatches.

5 If necessary, drag the Swatches palette by its tab so that it doesn't obscure the Layers palette.

6 Do one of the following:

• To fill the fish with color, click the Fill box in the toolbox.

• To outline the fish with color, click the Stroke box in the toolbox.

7 Click a swatch in the Swatches palette to select a color. (For more information on selecting colors and painting, see Lesson 4, "Painting.")

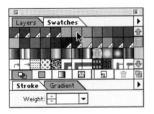

8 In the Layers palette, Command-click (Macintosh) or Ctrl-click (Windows) the eye icon next to the Drawing layer again to return to Artwork view.

Notice that the eye icon now appears hollow. You can press Command+Y (Macintosh) or Ctrl+Y (Windows) to return all of the artwork to Preview view.

9 Continue tracing over different parts of the fish to add more detail to the illustration. Practice tracing in Artwork view and painting in Preview view.

 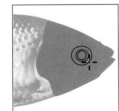

Artwork view   *Preview view*

You've completed the tracing lesson. For a lesson devoted just to layers, see Lesson 10, "Working with Layers."

 For additional tracing tips, take the "Hand-tracing in Illustrator" lesson in Module 4 of the online companion course.

Review

• How do you use placed artwork as an aid in creating new artwork?

You can place artwork on a new layer, dim the placed artwork, and then use any of the drawing tools to trace over the placed artwork.

• Name two graphic file formats you can use to import an image for tracing.

Illustrator can import and export many common graphic file formats, including GIF, JPEG, PICT, TIFF, PDF, and PostScript®.

• What is the difference between linking a placed file and embedding a placed file?

A placed file that is linked contains a reference to an external file, resulting in a smaller Illustrator file; however, the external file always must accompany the Illustrator file. A placed file that is embedded is included in the Illustrator file, resulting in a larger Illustrator file.

• How do you prevent all the objects on a layer from being selected or moved?

You can lock a layer to prevent objects on the layer from being selected or moved.

• Name two ways to lock a layer.

You can lock a layer using several techniques. (1) You can select the Lock option in the Layer Options dialog box. (2) You can click the blank column to the right of the eye icon and next to the layer; a pencil with a slash appears, indicating that the layer is locked. (3) You can also hide a layer to hide the objects on the layer and prevent them from being edited.

• Describe two ways to trace a placed image.

You can trace a placed image several ways. (1) Use the drawing tools, such as the pen tool (✿) and the pencil tool (✎). (2) Use the autotrace tool (✏). (3) Use a dedicated tracing program such as Adobe Streamline.

Lesson 8

Lesson 8

Creating Symmetrical Drawings

Using the reflect tool, you can create symmetrical shapes. You can then use the Average and Join commands to join shapes.

In this lesson, you'll learn how to

- Create a mirror image using the reflect tool
- Join line segments
- Move anchor points by averaging their line segments

Creating a mirror image

You'll use the reflect tool to make a mirror image of a shape. Reflecting an object flips the object across an invisible axis that you specify.

To begin working, you'll open an existing art file.

1 Choose File > Open, and locate and open the Symmetry.ai file in the Lesson08 folder. This folder is inside the Lessons folder in the AICIB folder on your hard drive.

Part of a vase is displayed.

(To see a sample of the finished artwork, open the Symmtry2.ai file in the Lesson04 folder, inside the Samples folder in the AICIB folder on your hard drive.)

2 Choose File > Save As, name the file Symmtry1.ai; then click Save.

3 Click the selection tool (➤) in the toolbox, and then click the outline to select it.

Now you'll use the reflect tool to make a mirror image of the shape.

4 Click the reflect tool (⬚) in the toolbox to select it.

5 Hold down Option (Macintosh) or Alt (Windows), and click the anchor point at the bottom of the vase.

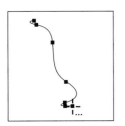

Like all of the transformation tools, the reflect tool performs its function in relation to some fixed point on or around the object. This fixed point is called the *origin of transformation*. The point of origin—indicated by a bull's eye icon—is the object's center point unless you click elsewhere with the reflect tool.

Holding down Option/Alt displays a cross hair next to the reflect tool pointer, indicating that clicking will open the Reflect dialog box so that you can specify precise values for the reflect operation.

6 Click Vertical, and then click Copy to duplicate the shape as it is reflected.

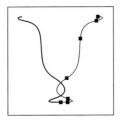

Reflecting an object about its vertical axis

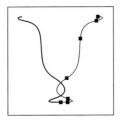

Result

Copying while reflecting lets you create a mirror image of an object.

You can also reflect an object by dragging. When you drag, the axis of reflection (that is, the point of origin) rotates around the point you click. For finer control over the reflection, drag farther from the object's point of origin.

Now you will extend the width of the vase by moving the reflected copy to the right.

7 Click the selection tool (➤) in the toolbox.

8 Begin dragging the copy to the right; then hold down Shift and continue dragging.

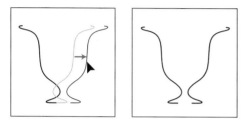

Holding down Shift constrains the movement to a horizontal direction.

9 Deselect the artwork by clicking away from it.

Joining anchor points

Next, you will create a path between the top anchor points using the Join command.

1 Click the direct-selection tool (▷).

Remember that to select individual anchor points, you must use the direct-selection tool.

2 Click one of the top anchor points.

3 Shift-click the other top anchor point to add it to the selection.

4 Choose Object > Path > Join to join the anchor points by a single line segment.

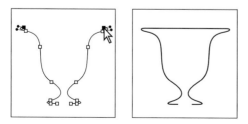

Because the endpoints aren't on top of each other, the Join command draws a path between the two points and closes the path. If the endpoints of a path coincide, the Join command replaces them with a single anchor point.

5 Deselect the artwork.

Averaging anchor points

The Average command lets you move two or more anchor points to a position that is the average of their current location.

Before you join the anchor points at the bottom of the vase, you'll use the Average command to move both points to the average position of their current location, and ensure that the points are precisely aligned and overlapping.

1 Using the direct-selection tool, drag a selection marquee (a dotted rectangle) to select the two anchor points at the bottom of the vase.

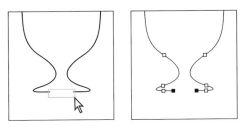

Note: You can switch between the selection tool and direct-selection tool by pressing Command+Tab (Macintosh) or Ctrl+Tab (Windows).

2 Choose Object > Path > Average. In the Average dialog box, select Both, and click OK. The two points are precisely aligned.

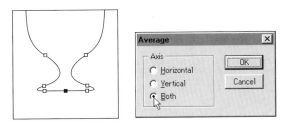

The Average command doesn't connect the anchor points; you can still select them and move them apart using the direct-selection tool.

Now you'll join the anchor points together and create a closed path.

3 With the anchor points still selected, choose Object > Path > Join, and click OK in the Join dialog box.

The path is now a single, closed shape.

4 Choose File > Close, save your changes if desired, and close the file.

You can create mirror images and add depth to them at the same time for a three-dimensional effect using the Adobe Dimensions® program. For an interactive demo of Adobe Dimensions, see the Adobe Tours folder on the Adobe Illustrator Tour and Training CD.

Review

• How do you reflect and copy a shape simultaneously?

You can reflect and copy two ways. (1) Using the reflect tool, Option-click (Macintosh) or Alt-click (Windows) to set the point of origin and display the Reflect dialog box; choose an axis of reflection and angle, and click Copy. (2) You can also reflect and copy an object with the reflect tool by clicking to set the point, and then Option-dragging or Alt-dragging to reflect and copy.

• How does the Join command differ from the Average command when applied to two anchor points at different locations?

The Join command draws a line between the two anchor points to connect them. The Average command moves the points together by averaging the distance, but does not join the anchor points—it only makes them coincident.

• Describe what the Join command does when one anchor point is positioned directly on top of another.

The Join command joins the two points to create a single anchor point.

Lesson 9

Lesson 9

Working with Type

One of the most powerful features of Adobe Illustrator is the ability to use type as a graphic element. You can quickly change type size, shape, and scale; you can precisely flow type into virtually any shape of object; and you can flow type horizontally or vertically along differently shaped paths. Adobe Illustrator also lets you paint type with colors, gradients, or patterns, and create type in a multitude of languages.

In this lesson, you'll learn how to do the following:

• Create type in a document, including along a path and vertically

• Set up a document for your page layout

• Import text

• Adjust type attributes and formatting, including the font, leading, and paragraph alignment

• Wrap type around a graphic

Much of the text you create in Illustrator will be short: a headline here, a word there. To learn more about cool type effects, take the "Point type" lesson in Module 5 of the online companion course.

Adding type to a document

You'll start the lesson by adding some type to an existing document.

1 Choose File > Open, and locate and open the Columns.ai file in the Lesson09 folder. This folder is located the Lessons folder within the AICIB folder on your hard drive.

(To see a sample of the finished artwork, open the Columns2.ai file in the Lesson09 folder in the Samples folder within the AICIB folder on your hard drive.)

2 Choose File > Save As, type the name Work09.ai; then click Save.

You'll add some teaser text above the Rock'n Roads headline.

3 Select the type tool (**T**). The small horizontal line near the bottom of the I-beam—its cross hair—marks the position of the type *baseline*.

The baseline is the line on which the type rests.

4 Position the pointer so that the I-beam cross hair is just above the Rock'n Roads headline. Use the guides that already exist in the document.

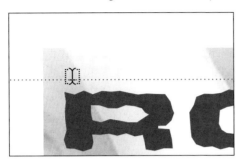

5 Click to set the type baseline.

6 Type **Weekend riding is not what it used to be**.

By default, the type you create is 12-point Helvetica, filled with black, and stroked with None. The Fill and Stroke boxes in the toolbox display the type's current paint attributes. We set the type to 20-point Frutiger Extra Black Condensed with 150 em letterspacing. You'll learn later in this lesson how to change type settings.

(For more information about selecting a fill or stroke color, see Lesson 4, "Painting," or see "Painting" [Chapter 9] in the *Adobe Illustrator User Guide* or in online Help.)

Another way to create type in Illustrator is to enter type along a path.

7 Position the pointer on the type tool in the toolbox, and drag to select the path-type tool (✎).

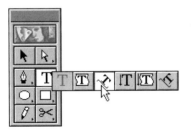

As a shortcut when the type tool is selected, press Option (Macintosh) or Alt (Windows) to get the path-type tool.

Now you'll add a photo credit to the curved path that outlines the bicycle wheel.

8 Position the path-type tool pointer on the curved line outlining the bicycle wheel.

9 Click to convert the line into a type path.

10 Type a credit for the photographer: **Photo by KT.**

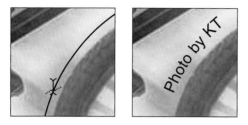

11 Command-click (Macintosh) or Ctrl-click (Windows) away from the type to deselect it.

Notice that the path no longer is painted. When you turn a path or object into a type path, the path becomes unstroked and unfilled, even if the path was originally stroked or filled. After you enter type, the type is selected, and any changes to the paint settings affect only the type, not the path.

12 To adjust the position of the type on the path, click the selection tool (▶), and click the type path if it is not already selected.

13 Position the pointer on the I-beam in the line of type. Press the mouse button and begin dragging the I-beam in the direction you want to move the type.

(Be careful not to drag across the path.)

Setting up a document

Next, you'll set up a document for the rest of your page layout, which will include columns of type and some graphics. You'll use the rulers to create guides.

The solid rectangle around this document represents the *page boundary*, the physical size of the page. The dotted rectangle represents the *imageable area*—what will print on the page—for the currently selected printer.

When designing a page, it's helpful to know its boundaries so that you can avoid surprises when you print your artwork. For now, you don't need to view the imageable area. You'll hide the imageable area boundary to more easily view the lines in your artwork.

1 Choose View > Hide Page Tiling.

Next, you'll use the rulers to create guides and to measure distances.

2 Choose View > Show Rulers to display rulers along the top and left side of the window. The ruler units in this document have been set to inches.

You can change the ruler unit of measure for all documents in the Units & Undo Preference dialog box, or for only the current document in the Document Setup dialog box. The ruler unit of measure applies to measuring objects, moving and transforming objects, setting grid and guide spacing, and creating ellipses and rectangles. It does not affect the units in the Character, Paragraph, and Stroke palettes. (The latter units are controlled by the Type option in the Units & Undo Preference dialog box.) To display the Units & Undo Preference dialog box, choose File > Preferences > Units & Undo. To display the Document Setup dialog box, choose File > Document Setup.

Now you'll create ruler guides to help you align artwork.

By default, rulers appear on the left side and at the top of the document window. The ruler origin is at the lower left corner of the page (0, 0). However, we prepared this file with the ruler origin set in the upper left corner and a Landscape orientation for better display on smaller monitors.

3 Position the pointer inside the left ruler, and drag across to the 3.5-inch mark on the top (horizontal) ruler to create the first vertical guide. Then drag down from the top (vertical) ruler to the 2.5-inch mark on the left ruler to create the second horizontal guide.

Drag vertical guide   *Drag horizontal guide*
from left ruler.   *from top ruler.*

You'll refer to the guides you just set and the rulers as you create a type container for your text.

The Character palette is the key feature to use when you want to format type. To explore more type formatting options, take the "Formatting type" and "Vertical type" lessons in Module 5 of the online companion course.

Creating columns of type

Now you'll create a type rectangle to use as a column of type.

1 Select the type tool (**T**), and position the pointer so that the I-beam cross hair is over the intersection of the guides.

2 Drag downward and to the right. As you drag, dotted lines appear in the ruler, indicating the pointer's coordinates.

When the pointer is at the 7.75-inch mark on the left ruler and the 10-inch mark on the top ruler, release the mouse button. Once you release the mouse button, the pointer reverts to an I-beam.

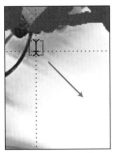

Position type tool at intersection of guides.

The text rectangle you just created is unpainted (neither filled nor stroked). When deselected, it is not visible in Preview view nor when you print it, unless you fill or stroke the text rectangle or you select type in it.

You no longer need the rulers or the guides.

3 Choose View > Hide Rulers and View > Hide Guides.

Next you'll convert this single type rectangle to three type containers that will each hold a column of type. You'll use the Rows & Columns command to divide the type block precisely.

4 Click the selection tool (**↖**) in the toolbox to automatically select the newly created type container.

5 Choose Type > Rows & Columns. This command is useful for changing the height and width of rows and columns and the gutter size between them.

The Text Flow option lets you control the direction in which text flows (from left to right or up and down). This option lets you easily use Illustrator to create designs using Chinese, Japanese, and Korean (CJK) and other non-Roman fonts.

6 Enter 3 in the Columns text box, leave the other values at their defaults, and click OK.

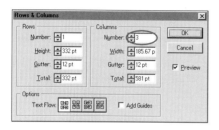

The three type containers are linked—so that text flows between containers—and grouped—so that selecting one container selects all three containers.

7 Before continuing, choose View > Artwork.

By switching to Artwork view, you can see the type containers even when they're not selected, and you can work more easily with type.

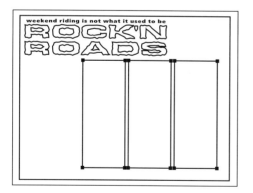

8 Select the type tool (**T**). The pointer changes to an I-beam within a dotted box.

9 Move the pointer to inside the left type container.

Make sure that the dotted rectangle around the pointer has disappeared so that the type will be entered within the rectangles.

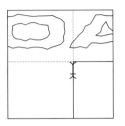

10 Click in the upper left of the first type container to set the text insertion point (the blinking cursor).

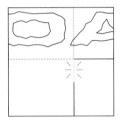

An outline appears around the text boxes in the same color as the layer color.

Next, you'll import text into the columns. You can import text as you would any other graphic object, using the Place command.

11 Choose File > Place. Select the Text file, located in the Columns folder, and click Place.

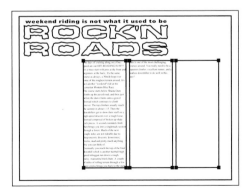

Illustrator supports more than a dozen text formats for the Macintosh and Windows, including Microsoft® Word and Rich Text Format (RTF), and WordPerfect®.

You can also bring text into Illustrator by copying and pasting text from the Clipboard. But the copied text loses its type attributes (such as its font and styles) when pasted into your document.

Setting type attributes

Next, you will format the type that you just imported. The Character palette has controls for setting the font and size, leading, kerning, and other type characteristics. The palette also has hidden options for horizontal and vertical scale, baseline shift, and language, which make it easy to design layouts using Chinese, Japanese, and Korean (CJK) and other non-Roman fonts.

1 To change the font of all three columns of text simultaneously, do one of the following:

• If the type containers are still selected, choose Edit > Select All.

• Click the selection tool (➤) to select all of the imported text automatically.

Once you create type, immediately clicking the selection tool in the toolbox lets you select all of the type and the type container and edit it as you would a graphic object.

2 Choose Type > Character to display the Character palette. The Character palette appears, grouped in front of the Paragraph palette and MM Design palette.

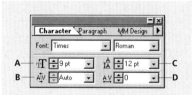

A. Type size B. Kerning C. Leading D. Tracking

By default, the Character palette displays the selected font and its style, size, kerning, leading, and tracking values. If the type selection contains two or more fonts, the Font text fields are blank. (*Leading* is the amount of space between lines or paragraphs. *Tracking* is the space in a string of characters.)

3 In the Character palette, choose Times Roman from the Font menu. Enter 9 in the Size text box and 12 in the Leading text box.

You can also adjust these options using individual Type menu commands.

4 Click away from the type to deselect it.

Next, you'll select the first paragraph and adjust it.

5 Select the type tool (**T**), and triple-click inside the first paragraph to select only that paragraph. (You can also select by dragging.)

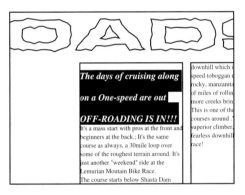

6 Experiment with different fonts and sizes and with different leading values. (We used Times Bold Italic at 13 points with 30 points of leading.)

You can set type attributes before you enter new type, or reset them to change the appearance of existing, selected type. If you select several type paths and type containers, you can set attributes for all of them at the same time.

Now you'll set the paragraph properties for all of the column text.

7 Using the selection tool (⬆) or pressing Command (Macintosh) or Ctrl (Windows), click the edge of the type container to select it.

8 Click the Paragraph tab next to the Character palette to display the Paragraph palette.

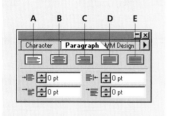

A. Align Left B. Align Center
C. Align Right D. Justify Full Lines
E. Justify All Lines

To use either the Paragraph or MM Design palette grouped with the Character palette, you click its tab to bring the palette to the front of its group.

9 In the Paragraph palette, select the Justify Full Lines option (the option second from the right).

10 Enter 10 in the Space Before Paragraph text box (the bottom right box) to separate paragraphs by 10 points of spacing.

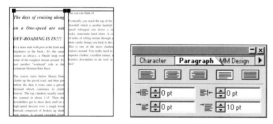

11 Command-click (Macintosh) or Ctrl-click (Windows) away from the artwork to deselect it.

Adjusting the text flow

Next, you'll shorten the first text container to fit the introductory paragraph and force the type to begin in the second container. Because the type containers are linked, adjusting any of the containers affects all of them and the type within them.

1 Click the direct-selection tool (⤵). Because type containers are grouped, you must use the direct-selection tool to select their parts.

2 Hold down Shift to constrain the move to a straight line, and drag the bottom of the left container up to the bottom of the first paragraph.

Notice how the type flows into the second container as you adjust it.

Type flows from one object to another based on the type containers' stacking order. Type flows first into the backmost object in the stacking order and continues to the next object in the stacking order. The most recently created object is frontmost. In this case, the stacking order is from left to right, in the order in which the containers were created.

3 Deselect the artwork by clicking away from it or by choosing Edit > Deselect All.

For more on flowing text into multiple columns, take the "Area text" lesson in Module 5 of the online companion course. Then explore another common use of type—creating tables—in the "Tabs and tables" lesson.

Wrapping type around a graphic

To complete the layout, you'll add a piece of artwork and wrap type around it.

1 Open the Wrap.ai file, located in the Lesson09 folder. The file contains a placed, linked EPS image with a pen tool path around it.

You can make type wrap around any graphic object in Illustrator. In this example, we've drawn a path around the placed image so that the type will wrap around the image.

2 Choose Edit > Select All and Edit > Copy to copy the image to the Clipboard. Then close the file.

3 Choose Edit > Paste to paste the image in front of the type. An object must be in front of type for type to wrap around it.

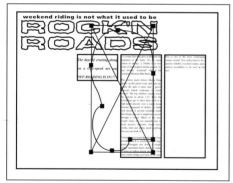

Paste object in front of type.

Because the document is in Artwork view, only the bounding box and an unpainted pen tool appear around the image.

4 Drag the pasted image to the upper right of the page.

5 Choose View > Preview to view the image and the unpainted path around it.

We added the unpainted path to create an editable boundary around the image and make it easy to adjust the type wrap.

6 Click the selection tool (↖), and Shift-click the square border of the image to deselect it.

7 Shift-click one of the type containers to select all three containers. The containers and the unpainted pen tool path around the image should be selected.

You must use area type when wrapping type around a path; point type and path type do not wrap around an object.

8 Choose Type > Wrap > Make to wrap the type around the path.

Select type and object to be wrapped.

Result

9 Zoom in on the front tire of the woman's bicycle.

Notice that the text wraps too closely to the bottom of the image. To see the path better, you'll switch to Artwork view.

10 Choose View > Artwork or press Command+Y (Macintosh) or Ctrl+Y (Windows). This shortcut switches between Artwork view and Preview view.

11 Click away from the artwork to deselect it.

By using an unpainted graphic boundary around your graphic object, you can adjust and resize the unpainted boundary to get the exact text wrap desired.

12 Select the direct-selection tool (κ), and drag the anchor point at the bottom of the path downward to adjust the text wrap.

Artwork view of wrapped type

13 Press Command+Y (Macintosh) or Ctrl+Y (Windows) to switch back to Preview view.

Changing type orientation

The range of type tools in Illustrator lets you flow type horizontally or vertically anywhere in a document.

1 Double-click the hand tool ($\text{\textsuperscript}$) to zoom out of the artwork. This shortcut fits the artwork in the window.

2 Using the type tool, click anywhere in the document and type **Special feature**.

Now you'll change the orientation of this type so that you can use it as a design element.

3 Click the selection tool (κ) in the toolbox to select the type you just created.

4 Choose Type > Type Orientation > Vertical. The type now flows vertically.

5 Drag the type to position it flush left with the first column of text.

You can use the Vertical orientation option to easily create designs using Japanese, Chinese, and Korean (CJK), and other fonts, or as a design element for Roman fonts. To reorient type horizontally, simply select it with the selection tool and choose Type > Type Orientation > Horizontal.

As a final step, you'll adjust the font of the "Special feature" text.

6 Click the Character palette tab to display the palette, and then choose a font and size. Press Enter to apply the change. (We used Helvetica Bold, 14 points.)

Some of the type attributes have separate submenus or palettes so that you don't have to open the Character or Paragraph palette if you want to change only one attribute. For more information, see "Setting type attributes" in Chapter 12 of the *Adobe Illustrator User Guide* or in online Help.

In addition, some attributes can be changed using keyboard shortcuts. For a complete list of shortcuts, see the *Adobe Illustrator Quick Reference Card*.

7 Command-click (Macintosh) or Ctrl-click (Windows) away from the artwork to deselect it.

8 Choose File > Close, save your changes if desired, and close the file.

For information on other features you can use when working with type, such as kerning, tracking, tabs, and searching, see "Using Type" (Chapter 13) in the *Adobe Illustrator User Guide* or in online Help.

 Take the "Converting text to graphics" lesson in Module 5 of the online companion course to learn how to create paths from character outlines.

Review

• How do you create guides in your artwork?

You display the rulers and use the selection tool pointer to drag guides from either the horizontal or vertical ruler.

• Describe two ways to create type in a document.

You can create type in various ways. (1) Use the type tool (**T**)to click and enter type at the point. (2) Use the path-type tool (↴) to convert any path in your artwork to a type path. (3) Use the type tool (**T**) to drag a type column and enter type within it. (4) Use the area-type tool (𝕋) to convert an object (like a circle) into a type block and then enter type in it.

• How do you get type into any of the type shapes you can create?

You import type using the Place command, or start typing.

• Describe the difference between the page boundary and imageable area. Why are they important?

The *page boundary* is the physical size of the page. The imageable area is what will print on the page for the currently selected printer. You should design your artwork within these boundaries.

• When you click with the type tool, where does it begin to create type?

Type begins at the cross hair of the type tool's I-beam pointer. The cross hair sets the baseline of the type.

• How do you convert a rectangle drawn with the rectangle tool into a series of columns?

Select the rectangle and apply the Type > Rows & Columns command.

• What controls the flow of text in type containers?

Type containers are linked, and text within them flows according to the stacking (painting) order. That is, the first-created container is backmost in the artwork; text flows from the backmost to the frontmost container. You can change the stacking order by using the Object > Arrange > Send to Back or Bring Forward command, or you can change the text flow by choosing Type > Rows & Columns.

• Name two tools you can use to adjust type attributes.

You can use the Character or Paragraph palette, individual commands in the Type menu, and keyboard shortcuts.

• Describe how to wrap type around an object.

Place the object around which the area type will wrap in front of the type. Create or use area type only, and select the type and the object. Choose Type > Wrap > Make. To wrap type precisely around an object, you can use an unpainted (no fill, no stroke) graphic drawn around the graphic object as the wraparound object.

• How do you make type flow vertically?

You select the type and choose Type > Type Orientation > Vertical.

Lesson 10

Lesson 10

Working with Layers

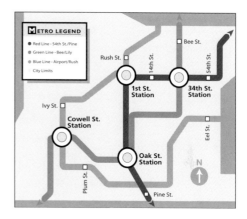

Layers let you organize your work into distinctive levels that can be edited and viewed as individual units. Every Adobe Illustrator document contains at least one layer. Creating multiple layers in your artwork lets you easily control how artwork is printed, displayed, and edited.

In this lesson, you'll learn how to do the following:

- Work with the Layers palette
- Create a new layer
- Rearrange layers
- Lock layers to preserve your artwork
- Paste layers from one file to another

Using the Layers palette

In this lesson, you'll start with a file that has already been organized into layers. You'll add a new layer and use the Layers palette to rearrange and edit the artwork.

1 Open the Layers.ai document in the Lesson10 folder. This folder is located the Lessons folder within the AICIB folder on your hard drive.

(To see a sample of the finished artwork, open the Layers2.ai file in the Lesson10 folder in the Samples folder within the AICIB folder on your hard drive.)

2 Choose File > Save As, type the name Work10.ai; then click Save.

3 If the Layers palette isn't visible on-screen, choose Window > Show Layers to display the Layers palette.

The Layers.ai document contains three layers; the layer at the top of the list contains the artwork on the frontmost layer, and the layer at the bottom of the list contains the artwork on the backmost layer. The selected layer is highlighted and has a pen icon, indicating that layer will be edited when you use the tools.

4 To see how the transit map artwork is organized, click the eye icon (the leftmost column next to the layer name) to hide that layer. The slash through the pen icon indicates that the hidden layer can't be edited.

A. Hide B. Unlock
C. Active layer D. Show

5 Then click again in the Show/Hide column to redisplay the layer.

Clicking the Show/Hide column (where the eye icon appears) switches between hiding and showing a layer.

6 Click the eye icon next to the various layers to turn the layers on and off and view different parts of the artwork.

You can also Command-click (Macintosh) or Ctrl-click (Windows) in the Show/Hide (leftmost) column to display an individual layer in Artwork view.

7 Command-click (Macintosh) or Ctrl-click (Windows) in the Show/Hide (leftmost) column.

This action alternately displays an individual layer in Artwork view and in Preview view.

8 Command/Ctrl-click again to return to Preview view.

9 If any layer is hidden, choose Show All Layers from the Layers palette menu.

A shortcut for displaying all layers or hiding all but the active layer is to Option-click (Macintosh) or Alt-click (Windows) the Show/Hide column in the Layers palette.

10 Then Option-click (Macintosh) or Alt-click (Windows) the Show/Hide column next to the Background layer name to select it and turn off all layers but the Background.

Creating a layer

In the next steps, you will create a new layer onto which you will copy the lines from the Background layer. Placing each element of the map on a separate layer lets you more easily select and edit individual elements.

1 Option-click (Macintosh) or Alt-click (Windows) the New Layer button at the bottom of the Layers palette to create a new layer and display the Layer Options dialog box.

You can also choose New Layer from the Layers palette menu. If you simply want to create a new layer without setting any options or naming the layer, you can click the New Layer button. New layers created this way are numbered in sequence (for example, Layer 4).

2 In the Layer Options dialog box, name the layer "Lines." Choose cyan (or another color) from the Color menu.

3 Click OK. The new layer appears at the top of the Layers palette and is selected.

Notice that the number of layers appears at the bottom of the Layers palette. The pen icon to the right of the layer name in the palette indicates the layer being edited. New objects you create or paste into the artwork are placed on the selected layer.

4 Click the selection tool (▸) in the toolbox, then click a line in the artwork. (The lines have been grouped, so that clicking one line selects all of them.)

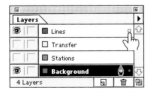

Selecting grouped lines also selects Background layer.   *Colored dot indicates selection is on Background layer.*

Because the selected lines are on the Background layer, the Background layer becomes active. The colored dot next to the pen icon on the Background layer indicates that the selected objects are on that layer.

5 Drag the colored dot up to the new layer, and release the mouse button when the dot appears next to the Lines layer.

Dragging the colored dot moves the selection to the new layer. (Option-dragging on the Macintosh or Control-dragging in Windows copies the selection rather than just moving it to the new layer.)

Notice that the anchor points and selected lines are cyan, the color you chose for the layer in step 2. Assigning different selection colors to layers makes it easier to distinguish artwork on different layers in the document.

Moving layers

You can also reorder layers in your artwork by rearranging the layers in the Layers palette.

1 Click the black triangle in the upper right corner of the Layers palette. You use this technique to access the Layers palette menu.

2 Choose Show All Layers from the Layers palette menu to redisplay all layers. Then click away from the artwork to deselect everything.

Notice that lines are on top of the map, obscuring the stations and transfer points.

3 Reposition the lines by dragging the Lines layer in the Layers palette to just below the Stations layer. Release the mouse button when the hand is between the Stations layer and the Background layer and a thick black line appears between the Stations and Background layers, indicating where the layer will be inserted.

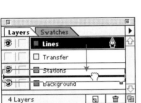

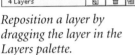

Reposition a layer by dragging the layer in the Layers palette.

You can select several layers at a time by Shift-clicking adjoining layers and Command-clicking (Macintosh) or Ctrl-clicking (Windows) nonsequential layers.

Locking layers

Now you will lock all the layers except the Stations layer so that you can easily edit the text on that layer without affecting objects on the other layers. Locked layers cannot be selected or edited in any way.

1 Click the Stations layer in the Layers palette to select the layer.

2 Choose Lock Others from the Layers palette menu to lock all other layers. The slash through the pencil icon indicates that a layer is locked.

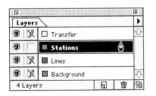

You can lock individual layers by clicking in the second column from the left in the Layers palette, called the Lock/Unlock column. Clicking again in the Lock/Unlock column unlocks the layer (the column appears blank).

3 In the Layers palette, Option-click (Macintosh) or Alt-click (Windows) the layer name to select everything on the Stations layer.

This is a shortcut for choosing Edit > Select All to select everything on the layer. Notice that nothing on the other layers is selected.

4 Choose Type > Character to display the Character palette. (You won't see a selection in the palette because the Stations layer uses more than one font.)

5 Select a different font from the Font menu.

6 Position the pointer next to the Stations layer name in the second column to the left, and Option-click (Macintosh) or Alt-click (Windows) to unlock all of the layers. The pencil icons with the slash through them disappear.

Option/Alt-clicking the Lock/Unlock column is a shortcut for switching between locking all layers but the selected layer and unlocking all layers. You can also choose Unlock All from the Layers palette menu to unlock all the layers.

Pasting layers

To complete the metro map, you'll copy and paste a key to the map from another file. You can paste a layered file into another file.

1 Open the Key.ai file, located in the Lesson10 folder. This folder is located in the Lessons folder in the AICIB folder on your hard drive.

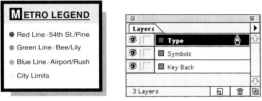

Key.ai file   Layers palette for Key.ai file

When you paste a layered file into another file, you can choose to paste the layers individually or to paste all the layers onto a single layer.

2 Choose Edit > Select All and then Edit > Copy to select and copy the key to the Clipboard; then close the file.

3 In the Layers.ai window, choose Paste Remembers Layers from the Layers palette menu. (A check mark should appear next to the command after you choose it.)

Turning on Paste Remembers Layers pastes the objects and keeps their layers intact. This option prevents the Paste commands from affecting layering; pasting then only affects the *stacking* or *painting order* of objects. (That is, the Adobe Illustrator program stacks successively drawn objects, beginning with the first drawn object.)

4 Choose Edit > Paste to paste the key into the map.

The Paste Remembers Layers command causes the Key layers to be pasted as three separate layers, at the top of the Layers palette.

5 Drag the Layers palette by its lower right corner to resize it to display all layers in the palette.

6 Click the selection tool (▶) in the toolbox, and drag the key into place at the top left corner of the map.

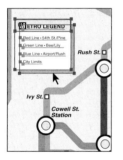

7 Deselect the artwork.

Merging layers

To streamline your artwork, you can *merge* layers. Merging layers combines the contents of all selected layers onto the top selected layer.

As a final step, you'll combine all artwork from the Key.ai file on one layer.

1 Select the Type, Symbols, and Key Back layers in the Layers palette.

2 Choose Merge Layers from the Layers palette menu.

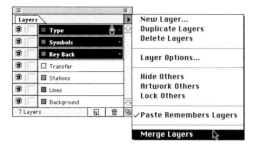

The objects on the merged layers retain their original painting order.

You can also minimize the file size by deleting layers you no longer need once you have finished editing your artwork and making design decisions. To delete a layer, simply select the layer and click the Trash button at the bottom of the Layers palette.

3 Choose File > Close, save your changes if desired, and close the file.

You have completed building a layered file. When you print a layered file, only the visible layers print, in the same order in which they appear in the Layers palette.

For a complete list of shortcuts that you can use with the Layers palette, see the *Adobe Illustrator Quick Reference Card*.

Review

• Name two benefits of using layers when creating artwork.

You can protect artwork that you don't want to change; you can hide artwork that you aren't working with so it's not distracting; you can control what prints.

• How do you hide layers? Display individual layers?

To hide a layer, you click the eye icon to the left of the layer name; you click in the blank, leftmost column to redisplay a layer.

• Describe how to reorder layers in a file.

You reorder layers by selecting a layer name in the Layers palette and dragging the layer to its new location. The order of layers in the Layers palette controls the document's layer order—topmost in the palette is frontmost in the artwork.

• How can you lock layers?

You can lock layers several different ways. (1) You can click in the column to the left of the layer name; a pencil with a slash through it appears, indicating that the layer is locked. (2) You can choose Lock Others from the Layers palette menu to lock all layers but the active layer. (3) You can hide a layer to protect it.

• What is the purpose of changing the selection color on a layer?

The selection color controls how selected anchor points and direction lines are displayed on a layer, and helps you identify the different layers in your document.

• What happens if you paste a layered file into another file? Why is the Paste Remember Layers command useful?

The Paste commands paste layered files or objects copied from different layers onto the same layer by default. The Paste Remembers Layers command pastes the objects and keeps their layers intact.

Beyond the Basics

In this section

Beyond the Basics is a collection of techniques for Adobe Illustrator users already familiar with the tools and features of Illustrator covered in the first section of this book. Beyond the Basics includes techniques for the following:

- Paint effects, including transparent effects, gradients, and path patterns
- Type masks
- Cutouts and interlocking shapes
- Isometric boxes, cylinders, and perspective drawing
- Creating color separations
- Creating artwork for the Web

The online course

The Web-based companion course from DigitalThink, *Mastering the Art*, is available for purchase from the DigitalThink Web site. The course offers intermediate to advanced lessons on the following topics:

- Module 1: Advanced Reshaping
- Module 2: Combining Paths
- Module 3: Type and Paths
- Module 4: Twisting and Turning
- Module 5: Gradations and Blends
- Module 6: Working with Photoshop

See page 3 for information on how to purchase the course, or point your web browser to http://www.digitalthink.com/partners/adobe/.

Lesson 11

Transparent Paint Effects

Let light and shadows into your artwork by simulating transparency using the Soft and Hard commands. The Soft command mixes the top color of overlapping shapes with the shapes underneath to create a new pseudo-transparent color. The Hard command mixes two or more colors to create a color that is a blend of the two.

In this lesson, you'll learn how to do the following:

• Create a transparent effect where the colors in artwork overlap

• Simulate transparency by overlapping objects and mixing their colors

• Select and edit objects created by the Soft and Hard Pathfinder commands

You can learn advanced techniques for working in Illustrator by enrolling in DigitalThink's online companion course, Mastering the Art. *This course expands upon topics covered in Beyond the Basics. See page 3. If you've already registered, get started by reading the course orientation and working through Module 1.*

Mixing colors using the Soft command

You can mix the colors in overlapping painted objects using the Hard and Soft Pathfinder commands. The Soft command lets you choose the amount of transparency in the resulting color.

The Soft command divides an image into its component faces and makes the top color of overlapping faces appear semitransparent. You specify the amount of color you want to show through overlapping objects.

1 Choose File > Open, and locate and open the Trnsprnt.ai file in the Lesson11 folder. This folder is located the Lessons folder within the AICIB folder on your hard drive.

(To see a sample of the finished artwork, open the Trnsprn2.ai file in the Lesson11 folder in the Samples folder within the AICIB folder on your hard drive.)

2 Choose File > Save As, type the name Work11.ai; then click Save.

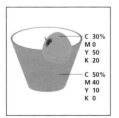

You'll use the Color palette to note the color values of the selected objects.

3 If the Color palette isn't visible on-screen, choose Window > Show Color.

4 Use the selection tool (➤) or direct-selection tool (➤) to select different objects in the artwork, and note their CMYK values in the Color palette.

5 Use the selection tool (➤) or direct-selection tool (➤) to select several overlapping objects whose colors you want to mix.

6 Choose Object > Pathfinder > Soft.

7 In the Soft dialog box, enter a Mixing Rate value for the percentage of transparency, and click OK.

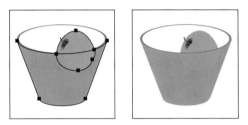

If you overlap multiple objects, each object is given the level of transparency you select. A low value produces a low level of transparency; a high value produces a high level of transparency.

The higher the rate, the more opaque the effect and the more the colors mix. We used a rate of 80%.

8 Deselect the artwork.

Now you'll use the eyedropper tool to sample the paint settings of the overlapping shape. (If you use the eyedropper tool without deselecting the artwork, the eyedropper applies the color it samples to all selected objects.)

9 Using the eyedropper tool (✐), click the overlapping shape. Note the new process mix of the overlapping shape in the Color palette.

Applying either the Hard or Soft Pathfinder command can alter the color mode of the objects. For example, if you select objects containing both spot colors and process colors, the artwork and the mixed colors will be converted to CMYK process color when you apply the Hard or Soft command. (If the objects are exclusively process colors, the mixed color retains the original color mode.) The Hard and Soft commands do not affect the color mix of gradient fills.

10 To select shapes created by the Soft command, use the direct-selection tool ().

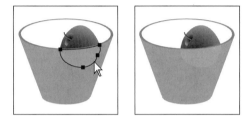

To vary the color effect, you can manually adjust the colors of the new shape using the sliders in the Color palette.

Simulating transparency using the Hard command

The Hard command mixes two or more colors from overlapping objects. This command is useful for approximating the colors on overprinted objects. Overprinting makes overlapping printing inks appear transparent. (By default, both fills and strokes in the Adobe Illustrator program appear opaque because the top color *knocks out*, or cuts out, the area underneath.)

The Hard command, like the Soft command, divides objects into separate shapes.

In the next few steps, you'll add a tablecloth and drop shadow to the apple bowl art. (We created the bowl of apples by copying the apple in the Trnsprnt.ai artwork several times and changing the bowl's fill to a stroke.)

1 For the tablecloth, create the first stripe by drawing a rectangle next to the bowl of apples. If you want to simulate perspective, use the shear tool (⧄) to shear the rectangle.

2 To create additional stripes for the tablecloth, select the rectangle and Option-drag (Macintosh) or Alt-drag (Windows) it to the right to copy the rectangle, holding down Shift to keep the copy perfectly horizontal.

Choose Object > Transform > Transform Again (Command+D on the Macintosh or Ctrl+ D in Windows) to create additional stripes as desired.

Select all of the stripes and fill them with a color. Then choose Object > Arrange > Send Backward to position the stripes behind the bowl.

3 For the drop shadow, use a drawing tool to create a shape for the drop shadow, and choose Object > Arrange > Send Backward to position it behind the bowl.

4 To fill the shadow, select a grayscale value in the Color palette or Swatches palette, or for a more realistic effect, fill the shadow with color (for example, the color of the object casting the shadow).

Then use the HSB color mode and sliders in the Color palette to adjust the saturation of the color, or use the Colors > Saturate filter. (For more information, see "Desaturating colors" on page 81 or see the online Help topic.)

Now you'll mix the colors in the overlapping objects you just created.

5 Using the selection tool (▶), Shift-click to select all of the overlapping objects (in this case, the stripes and drop shadow) to which you will apply the hard mix effect.

6 Choose Object > Pathfinder > Hard.

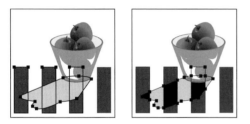

The Hard command combines the highest CMYK value from each color in the selection to create a new color mix.

For example, if Color 1 is created from 20% C, 66% M, 40% Y, and 0% K; and Color 2 is created from 40% C, 20% M, 30% Y, and 10% K; the resulting hard mix color is 40% C, 66% M, 40% Y, and 10% K.

If your selection includes both spot and process colors, the resulting mixed color will be the combined highest CMYK value from each color in the selection.

7 If you want to select the shapes created by the Hard command, use the direct-selection tool (⬀).

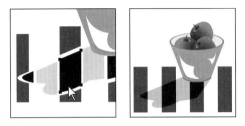

To vary the effect, you can adjust the color mix by hand using the sliders in the Color palette.

8 Choose File > Close, save your changes if desired, and close the file.

See the following topics for more information:

• For more information about painting objects, see Lesson 4, "Painting."

• For more information about color modes and overprinting, see Lesson 21, "Printing Artwork and Producing Color Separations."

• For more information about creating transparent effects when printing, see "Producing Color Separations" (Chapter 16) in the *Adobe Illustrator User Guide* or in the online Help.

• For more information about the Hard and Soft commands, see "Painting" (Chapter 9) in the *Adobe Illustrator User Guide* or in the online Help.

Review

• Describe two uses for the Hard and Soft commands.

The Hard and Soft commands mix colors in overlapping objects. You can use the commands to simulate transparency or to simulate overprinting on-press. You can also use the commands to divide overlapping objects into their component parts.

• What happens if you apply the Soft or Hard command to an object painted with a spot color and an object painted with a process color?

Applying either the Soft or Hard command to multiple objects that have more than one color mode converts the artwork's color mode to CMYK.

• How do you select objects to which you have applied the Hard or Soft command?

You must use the direct-selection tool. Both the Hard and Soft commands divide overlapping objects into component faces.

Lesson 12

Lesson 12

Creating Cutouts

You can use the Exclude and Divide Path-finder commands to create cutout shapes. These cutouts act as a window into your artwork. Which command you use depends on the effect you want.

In this lesson, you'll learn to

• Create cutouts where shapes overlap

• Create new shapes where shapes overlap

• Select and edit compound paths to create the appearance of transparency in your artwork

Explore advanced tips and techniques for using the Pathfinder filters by taking the "Introducing the Pathfinder filters," "Subtracting shapes from each other," and "Combining many paths into one" lessons in Module 2 of the online companion course, Mastering the Art. *See page 3.*

Creating cutouts from overlapping shapes

The Pathfinder commands let you combine, isolate, and subdivide paths, as well as build new objects formed by the intersection of objects.

You'll start by using the Exclude Pathfinder command.

1 To use the artwork shown here, choose File > Open, and locate and open the Cutout.ai file in the Lesson12 folder. This folder is inside the Lessons folder in the AICIB folder on your hard drive.

(To see a sample of the finished artwork, open the Cutout2.ai file in the Lesson12 folder, inside the Samples folder in the AICIB folder on your hard drive.)

If you want to use your own artwork, start with a shape, and draw another shape within the boundaries of the first shape.

2 Choose File > Save As, name the file Cutout1.ai; then click Save.

Original

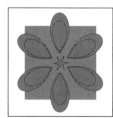

Interior shapes added

3 Using the selection tool (➤), click one of the petals in the Exclude artwork. All shapes, except the rectangle, should be selected.

We grouped all of the petals in the artwork to make it easier to see the effect of the Exclude command.

4 Choose Object > Pathfinder> Exclude. The Exclude command traces all nonoverlapping areas of the selected objects and makes the overlapping areas transparent.

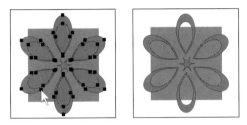

5 Deselect the artwork.

Where shapes overlapped, the Exclude command creates cutouts. These shapes are *compound paths*—that is, they have transparent interior spaces. Compound paths consist of two or more overlapping objects combined into a single compound object. Most of the Pathfinder commands create compound paths.

6 To edit or repaint individual shapes, use either the direct-selection tool (➤) or the group-selection tool (➤⁺) to select and edit them.

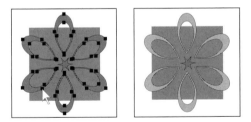

Because compound paths are grouped objects, you must use either the direct-selection tool or the group-selection tool to select part of the path. You can see that these shapes are compound paths, because if you reposition the shapes, they remain cutouts only where they overlap.

You can create even more complex compound paths using the Compound Paths command. For more information, see "Working with compound paths" in Chapter 7 of the *Adobe Illustrator User Guide* or in the online Help.

Creating new shapes from overlapping shapes

If you want to retain and edit an interior shape created from intersecting shapes, you can use the Divide command instead of the Exclude command to create new shapes from the overlapping shapes.

1 Start with shapes that overlap each other.

2 Using the selection tool (➤), click a petal in the Divide artwork to select all of the overlapping shapes.

Note: You can use the keyboard to switch to the selection tool when the group-selection tool is selected by pressing Command+Tab (Macintosh) or Ctrl+Tab (Windows).

Like the Exclude artwork, the petals in the Divide artwork are grouped to make it easier to see the effect of the Divide command.

3 Choose Object > Pathfinder > Divide.

The Divide command divides a piece of artwork into its component filled faces (a face is an area undivided by a line segment). The resulting faces can then be ungrouped and manipulated independently of each other.

4 Deselect the artwork.

Original　　　*Divide command applied*

Where shapes overlapped, the Divide command creates separate, grouped shapes that can be edited.

Note: *By default, any unfilled objects remaining in the selected artwork are deleted when you apply the Divide or the Outline command. To retain the objects, choose Object > Pathfinder > Options, and deselect the Divide and Outline will Extract Unpainted Artwork option.*

5 Using either the direct-selection tool (🔧) or the group-selection tool (🔧⁺), select one of the new shapes.

Because these shapes are grouped, you must use one of the specialized selection tools to select and edit the new shapes. (You can also select the entire group and ungroup it.)

6 Paint the new shapes as desired.

7 To achieve a cutout effect, you can also select and delete some of the shapes created by the Divide command.

New shapes repainted　　*New shapes deleted*

8 Choose File > Close, save your changes if desired, and close the file.

Review

• Describe the purpose of the Exclude command.

You use the Object > Pathfinder > Exclude command to make cutouts.

• Describe the purpose of the Divide command.

You use the Object > Pathfinder > Divide command to create new shapes from overlapping ones.

Compound paths are transparent where they overlap, so you can use them to create cutouts and windows into your artwork.

• What tool do you use to select and edit shapes that have been created using Divide and Exclude command?

You must use the direct-selection tool (⬚).

Lesson 13

Lesson 13

Interlocking Shapes

You can create interlocking objects using the Pathfinder Divide command to break up overlapping shapes into separate, distinct ones. Then repaint the shapes to make them appear to wind around one another. You can also make a shape seem to adhere to another by positioning shapes on top of each other and applying the Intersect command.

In this lesson, you'll learn to:

• Make objects appear to wind around shapes

• Make shapes follow the contours of another shape

• Combine overlapping objects

Creating realistic drop shadows can be tricky when you're working with overlapping shapes. Find out how to use the Hard and Soft commands to create shadows by taking the "Mixing colored shapes together" lesson in Module 2 of the online companion course, Mastering the Art. *See page 3.*

Interlocking shapes

As you saw in Lesson 12, "Creating Cutouts," when you overlap shapes and apply the Divide command, you create new shapes. You can use this technique to give depth to your artwork and make objects appear to wind around shapes or to intersect shapes.

1 Choose File > Open, and locate and open the Intrlock.ai file in the Lesson 13 folder. This folder is located in the Lessons folder within the AICIB folder on your hard drive.

(To see a sample of the finished artwork, open the Intrlck2.ai file in the Lesson13 folder, inside the Samples folder in the AICIB folder on your hard drive.)

You can also start with two separate objects.

2 Choose File > Save As, name the file Intrlck1.ai; then click Save.

3 To retain the original artwork, copy the objects and paste them elsewhere in your file.

4 Using the selection tool (➤), position the objects so that they overlap each other.

Original objects   *Objects repositioned to overlap*

5 Select both of the overlapping objects.

6 Choose Object > Pathfinder > Divide to divide the objects where they overlap into separate, distinct shapes.

The Divide command divides the selected shapes where they overlap, retains shapes that don't overlap, and groups the shapes it creates. You use the direct-selection tool to select individual shapes.

7 If the result is too complex, you can reunite shapes that you don't plan to edit by using the direct-selection tool (⬐) to select them, and choosing Object > Pathfinder > Unite.

The Unite command traces the outline of all selected objects as if they were a single, merged object, and deletes any objects inside the selected objects.

8 To complete the effect, use the direct-selection tool (⬐) to click a shape that will appear behind the tree.

9 Then select the eyedropper tool (✐) and click the shape (the tree) that will appear in front to sample its color and repaint the segment of the snake.

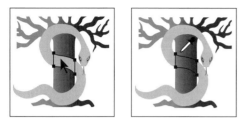

The eyedropper tool samples the paint attributes underneath the tool pointer, and applies them to any selected objects. If nothing is selected, you can press Option (Macintosh) or Alt (Windows) to get the paintbucket tool, and then click an object to paste the sampled paint attributes.

10 Repeat for other shapes as desired.

11 Choose File > Close, save your changes if desired, and close the file.

Intersecting shapes

Another way to intertwine shapes is to use the Intersect command to join two separate objects as one.

1 Choose File > Open, and locate and open the Intrsect.ai file in the Lesson 13 folder. This folder is located in the Lessons folder within the AICIB folder on your hard drive.

(To see a sample of the finished artwork, open the Intrlck2.ai file in the Lesson13 folder, inside the Samples folder in the AICIB folder on your hard drive.)

You can also use your own artwork and start with two separate objects.

2 Choose File > Save As, name the file Intrsct1.ai; then click Save.

3 Copy the objects and paste them elsewhere in your file to retain the original shapes for use in steps 3 through 7.

4 Option-drag (Macintosh) or Alt-drag (Windows) the artwork that you want to overlap into position. (Option- or Alt-dragging creates a copy of the original.) We overlapped a copy of the turquoise diamond on the snake's back.

Next, you'll copy the background around which the detail will wrap so that you can retain the background after applying the Intersect command. The Intersect command deletes any shapes that don't overlap.

5 Select the background object (we selected the snake) and choose Edit > Copy to copy it. Choose Edit > Paste in Back to make a copy of the background.

6 Shift-click to select the objects that will intersect. We selected the turquoise diamond and the snake's yellow body.

7 Choose Object > Pathfinder > Intersect to create an intersection of common shapes and delete any uncommon shapes.

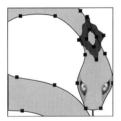 

Overlapping objects   *Intersect command applied*

The Intersect command traces the outline of all overlapping shapes in the selected objects, and deletes any nonoverlapping areas. This command works on only two objects at a time. Unlike the Divide command, the Intersect command doesn't retain nonoverlapping shapes.

8 To complete the intersecting shape, continue to repeat steps 3 through 6:

• Option/Alt-drag the overlapping artwork into position.

• Select the background and choose Edit > Copy and Edit > Paste in Back to paste a copy of the background shape behind the overlapping shape.

• Shift-click to select the objects that will intersect.

• Then reapply the Intersect command.

Overlapping objects   *Final result*

We rotated the diamond pattern as we reapplied it to the snakeskin. You can also scale or distort the object that you paste before you apply the Intersect command.

9 Choose File > Close, save your changes if desired, and close the file.

 You can use the Intersect and Divide commands to isolate areas where selected paths overlap. Take the "Finding the intersection of shapes" lesson in Module 2 of the online companion course, Mastering the Art. *See page 3.*

Review

• What effects do the Divide and Intersect commands have on overlapping shapes?

Both commands break up overlapping shapes into distinct shapes. The Divide filter retains any shapes that don't overlap, whereas the Intersect filter deletes any non-overlapping shapes.

• Describe a use for the Unite command.

If artwork contains many separate elements or is very complex, you can use the Unite filter to combine the overlapping elements into a single shape and simplify the artwork.

Lesson 14

Lesson 14

Creating Type Masks

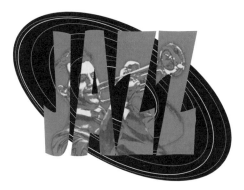

You can use any type as a mask without having to convert the type to outlines first. After creating a mask using type, you can still edit it—for example, by adjusting the font or size—and even type in new text.

In this lesson, you'll learn to:

• Mask artwork with type

• Edit the type mask

Creating a type mask

Masks crop part of an image so that only a portion of it is revealed through the shape or shapes that you create. You'll start with your own artwork that will show through the mask, or open an existing file that has been prepared for you.

1 To use the artwork shown here, choose File > Open, and locate and open the Typemask.ai file in the Lesson14 folder. This folder is located the Lessons folder within the AICIB folder on your hard drive.

(To see a sample of the finished artwork, open the Typmask2.ai file in the Lesson14 folder, inside the Samples folder in the AICIB folder on your hard drive.)

2 Choose File > Save As, name the file Typmask1.ai; then click Save.

3 If you're using your own artwork, select the artwork for the mask, and then position the artwork behind the type by choosing Object > Arrange > Send to Back.

The object that will be the mask can be single shape, multiple shapes, or text. The masking object must be must be on top of the artwork you want to mask.

4 Select the type and the artwork for the mask.

If you're masking objects on different layers, keep in mind that objects on intermediate layers become part of the masked artwork.

5 Choose Object > Masks > Make to convert the front object into a mask and see through to the artwork.

The mask loses its paint attributes and is assigned a fill and stroke of None. Thus, the mask isn't visible in Preview view unless you select it or assign it new paint attributes.

Put your type skills into high gear by exploring the powerful combination of type and paths. Take "Advanced type effects" in Module 3 of the online companion course, Mastering the Art. *See page 3.*

Editing a mask

Once you have created a mask, you can still adjust the artwork and the type (the mask) independently. For example, you can resize either the artwork (here, a placed photo) or the type, as well as rotate, skew, and reflect them.

1 To reposition the artwork within the mask, select just the artwork (photo), and make the desired adjustment. Here, we rotated the placed photo.

Although most of the artwork (the photo) isn't visible, its bounding area is still recognized by Illustrator. So you can click anywhere outside the type to select just the photo. You can also switch to Artwork view to see the photo's outlines. (Press Command+Y on the Macintosh or Ctrl+Y in Windows to switch between Preview and Artwork view.)

In addition, you can add an object to the masked artwork, or remove objects from the mask, using the selection tool to select parts of the masked artwork.

2 Select the type, and then choose a new font and size for the type.

Because the mask is still type (and not an object), you can adjust its font, style, size, alignment, kerning, and so on. You can even edit or retype the text.

3 Choose File > Close, save your changes if desired, and close the file.

For more information on selecting and editing masks, see "Working with masks" in Chapter 7 of the *Adobe Illustrator User Guide* or in online Help.

Review

• Where must the masking object be positioned in the artwork when you create a mask?

The masking object (mask) must be on top of the artwork that you want to mask.

• Why is a mask not visible?

The Make Masks command strips the mask of its paint attributes and assigns the mask a fill and stroke of None. The mask isn't visible unless you select it with the direct-selection tool (⬚) or assign it new paint attributes.

• How do you edit artwork in the mask?

You use the selection tool to select parts of the masked artwork, and then edit it as you would any Illustrator artwork.

Lesson 15

Lesson 15

Distributing Objects Around a Circle

You can distribute text and objects evenly around a circle using the rotate tool and some simple math.

In this lesson, you'll learn to

- Use an object's center point to align objects
- Use the rotate tool to align and copy objects
- Convert objects to guides for use as alignment tools
- Align type as you create it
- Rotate objects as you align them
- Repeat a rotation

Explore more of the transformation tools, and learn a few tricks for duplicating objects in a series in the online companion course, Mastering the Art. *Work through the transformation-related lessons to the duplicating series lesson in Module 4. See page 3.*

Arranging objects around a circle

You'll start by creating the object—a clockface—around which you will distribute objects—its numbers.

1 Choose File > Open, and locate and open the Circle.ai file in the Lesson 15 folder. This folder is located the Lessons folder within the AICIB folder on your hard drive.

(To see a sample of the finished artwork, open the Circle2.ai file in the Lesson15 folder, inside the Samples folder in the AICIB folder on your hard drive.)

2 Choose File > Save As, name the file Circle1.ai; then click Save.

3 Choose View > Artwork. It's easier to align objects when only the outlines are visible.

4 If you want to create your own artwork, draw a large circle for the clock face. Draw a smaller circle about the size of the numbers, and align its center point at the top of the large circle.

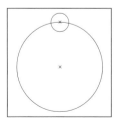

You use the center point to help you align objects.

5 Choose Edit > Select All. You must select artwork to be able to display its center point.

6 If the center points aren't visible in Artwork view, choose Window > Show Attributes to display the Attributes palette, and select the Show Center option.

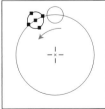

Show Center option

7 Using the selection tool (⬉), select the smaller circle.

8 Select the rotate tool (↻).

By default, objects rotate around the object's center point. You will designate another point of rotation by clicking with the rotate tool in the artwork.

9 Position the rotate tool on the center point of the larger circle, and Option-click (Macintosh) or Alt-click (Windows). Option/Alt-clicking with the rotate tool displays the Rotate dialog box.

10 In the Rotate dialog box, determine the placement of objects by dividing the circle's degrees, 360°, by the number of objects around it. (We divided 360° by 12 for an Angle of 30°.)

11 Enter that number, 30, in the Angle text box and click Copy.

12 Choose Object > Transform > Transform Again to repeat the rotation and copy for the desired number of copies. The keyboard shortcut for the Transform Again command is Command+D (Macintosh) or Ctrl+D (Windows).

Creating first rotated object

Rotating and copying to complete distribution

Copying while rotating is a useful way to create radially symmetrical objects. Next, you'll convert your artwork to guides to make it easier to align type.

13 Using the selection tool (➤), select just the small circles by Shift-clicking them. Choose Object > Group to group them so that you can easily select and edit them as a unit later.

14 Select the large circle and the smaller ones, and choose View > Make Guides > to convert the artwork to guides. Make sure that the View > Lock Guides command is selected (indicated by a checkmark in front of the command).

By default, objects within 2 pixels of guides snap to them.

15 Choose File > Preferences > General, and deselect the Snap to Point option so that objects don't snap to the guides. Click OK. (The guides are for visual alignment only.)

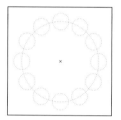

Aligning type

Now you'll complete the clock artwork by adding the numbers to the clockface. You can align type as you create it using the Alignment options. You can align the type either before or after you create it.

1 To align the numbers vertically around the circle, choose Type > Paragraph, and in the Paragraph palette, choose the Align Center option.

Align Center option

The Align Center option aligns the type from the center, even if you change the type's font and size.

2 Use the type tool to create the individual numbers. Either click the type tool in the toolbox, or Command-click (Macintosh) or Ctrl-click (Windows) after each number that you create.

By deselecting type after you create it, each piece of type you created acts as a separate object.

3 Using the selection tool, position the numbers manually within each guide. You can use the arrow keys to nudge the numbers in the corresponding direction 1 pixel at a time.

Center-aligned type   *Positioning type within guide*

You align the type separately from the rotation operation, because rotating and copying the type also would rotate its baseline.

Now you will group the numbers so that you can easily change their point size or font.

4 Choose Edit > Select All to select all of the numbers, and choose Object > Group to group them.

5 Choose Type > Character to display the Character palette.

6 In the Character palette, select another font or size for the group of numbers. (We used Pepita 60 pt.)

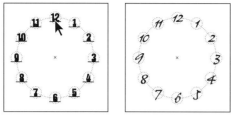

All type selected   Font changed globally

Because you chose the Align Center option, you don't have to realign the type visually after you change the font and size.

You can transform and edit guides as you would objects.

7 If you want to adjust the size of the guides, do the following:

• Deselect the Lock Guides command. (Choose View > Lock Guides to unlock the guides; the checkmark should disappear.)

• Select the group of small circles and choose Object > Transform > Transform Each.

• Select the Preview option, and enter a new horizontal or vertical scale, or both; when you are satisfied with the scale, click OK.

• When you have finished scaling the guides, choose View > Lock Guides to lock them again.

Distributing objects

When you rotate symmetrical objects like circles around artwork, it's not obvious that they are rotating. Now you will rotate artwork around a circle so that you can see the rotation, and then rotate additional objects in relation to the first rotation. This technique is similar to the first.

1 Working in Artwork view, draw a large circle. Draw a smaller object, and align its center point at the top of the large circle.

(If the center points aren't visible in Artwork view, select the objects, choose Window > Show Attributes, and select the Show Center option.)

2 With the small object selected, use the rotate tool (⟳) and Option-click (Macintosh) or Alt-click (Windows) the center point of the larger circle.

3 In the Rotate dialog box, determine the placement of objects by dividing the circle's degrees, 360°, by the number of objects around it (here, 72° for five planets). Click Copy to rotate and copy the first object.

4 Choose Object > Transform > Transform Again or press Command+D (Macintosh) or Ctrl+D (Windows) to position copies around the rest of the circle.

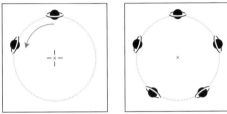

First copy rotated   *Object rotated and*
by 72°   *copied again*

You can use the Transform Again command to repeat a move, scale, rotate, reflect, or shear operation as many times as you want. You must choose the command immediately after you perform the operation.

Now you'll distribute a second object to the circle.

5 To align a second object (the moon), overlap it on top of an existing object. Then using the rotate tool, Option-click (Macintosh) or Alt-click the center point of the larger circle.

6 In the Rotate dialog box, rotate the overlapping object by half the angle used for the first object (here, 36°) to center it between the two objects. Click OK.

Now you will copy the object as you continue to rotate it.

7 Repeat steps 2 and 3, using the first angle of rotation (72°) to rotate and copy the second set of objects.

Second object rotated   *Second object rotated*
between originals   *and copied*

8 Press Command+D (Macintosh) or Ctrl+D (Windows) as many times as needed to repeat the Transform Again and position the remaining copies around the rest of the circle.

9 Choose File > Close, save your changes if desired, and close the file.

You can also rotate objects in a selection around its own centerpoint and rotate objects randomly using the Random option in the Transform Each dialog box. For more information, see "Rotating" in Chapter 7 of the *Adobe Illustrator User Guide* or in the online Help.

Review

• How do you determine the placement of objects around a circle? Around a semicircle?

You divide the number of objects that you want to distribute by the number of degrees in a circle (360°) or in a semicircle (180°). Then use the rotate tool to rotate the objects into position.

• How do you quickly repeat a rotation and copy?

Use the Object > Transform > Transform Again command.

- How do you display an object's center point, and why is it useful?

You select the object, choose Window > Show Attributes, and select the Show Center option. You can use the center point to align objects.

- What is the purpose of locking and then unlocking guides?

Locking guides prevents them from being moved; unlocking guides lets you edit them.

Lesson 16

Lesson 16

Drawing in Perspective

You can use guides and the transformation tools to help you create perspective drawings. To create perspective, you scale objects, setting the origin of the scaling at the vanishing point. Try creating other perspective grids that vary the horizon and vanishing point, and experiment with different scale percentages.

In this lesson, you'll learn how to do the following:

- Draw a perspective grid
- Convert a drawing to guides
- Make objects seem to recede into the background
- Uniformly scale objects for a perspective effect
- Blend objects

Creating a grid

You'll start by drawing a perspective grid. You'll use this grid as a template to create the artwork and align objects horizontally and vertically.

1 Choose File > Open, and locate and open the 3D.ai file in the Lesson16 folder. This folder is located in the Lessons folder in the AICIB folder on your hard drive.

(To see a sample of the finished artwork, open the 3D2.ai file in the Lesson16 folder, inside the Samples folder in the AICIB folder on your hard drive.)

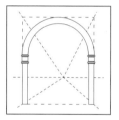

You'll refer to this artwork as you begin drawing a perspective grid.

2 Choose File > Save As, name the file Work1.ai; then click Save.

3 Using the pen tool (✎), draw a simple perspective grid with 1-point stroked lines. Include a picture plane (1), horizon line (2), and vanishing point (3).

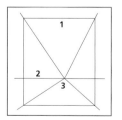

You can also use existing artwork as a guide. To turn artwork into guides, select it and choose View > Make Guides. You can then draw your artwork on top of the guides.

4 Using the selection tool (⬍), Shift-click to select the lines. Choose View > Make Guides to convert them to guides.

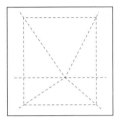

For easy alignment, you'll make sure that the Snap to Point option is selected so that the pointer will "snap" to the guides.

5 Choose File > Preferences > General. Select the Snap to Point option, and click OK.

6 Use the drawing tools to create the foreground objects.

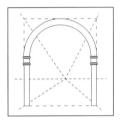

Now you'll create additional guides as needed. For example, you can create guides for aligning detail on the column sides.

7 Start from the vanishing point, and draw lines that intersect the corresponding (matching) points on the face of each column.

8 Select the lines, and choose View > Make Guides to convert those lines to guides.

9 Using the guides and their angle as a reference, draw the column sides in perspective.

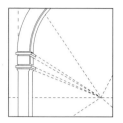

10 When you've drawn all the foreground objects, select all of the objects, and choose Object > Group to group them. Grouping objects lets you select and edit them as a unit.

Making objects recede

To make objects recede into the background, you'll use the scale tool.

1 Select the column, including any detail that you've added to it.

2 Click the scale tool (⊟) in the toolbox.

Scaling an object enlarges or reduces it horizontally (along the *x* axis) or vertically (along the *y* axis), or both horizontally and vertically, relative to the point of origin you designate. (The point of origin is the fixed point on or around the object from which the scaling occurs.)

3 Option-click (Macintosh) or Alt-click (Windows) the vanishing point of the drawings.

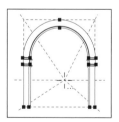

You can scale by dragging or using the Scale dialog box. Option/Alt-clicking with the scale tool displays the Scale dialog box so that you can precisely scale an object. (You can also scale precisely using the menu command; choose Object > Transform > Scale.) Unless you click elsewhere, the default point or origin is the object's center point.

4 In the Scale dialog box, click Uniform from the menu.

The Uniform option maintains the proportions of the original selection when scaling.

5 Enter a percentage. (We used 60%.) Select the Scale Line Weight option.

When you scale line weights, the line weights of all stroked paths (as specified in the Stroke palette) are scaled along with the objects.

6 Click Copy to make the selection seem to recede into the background.

7 Choose Object > Transform > Transform Again to repeat the scale and copy operation until you've created the effect you want. The shortcut for repeating a transformation such as scaling is Command+D (Macintosh)or Ctrl+D (Windows).

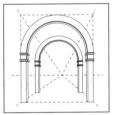 

Scale selected column by 60%.   *Repeat transformation.*

Build on your understanding of duplication series to create perspective effects. Take the "Creating perspective effects" lesson in Module 4 of the online companion course, Mastering the Art. *See page 3.*

Blending objects to make them recede

Another way to make objects recede into the background is to use the blend tool.

Now you'll create rows of evenly spaced floor tiles, as shown in this example. You'll start by drawing additional lines to act as guides for the tiles.

1 Using the pen tool (✒), draw two additional lines that intersect at the vanishing point. Then draw a horizontal line above the bottom of the picture plane.

2 Using the selection tool (▶), Shift-click the lines you just drew. Choose View > Make Guides to convert them to guides.

3 Using the pen tool (✒), draw the front left and right floor tiles in the areas defined by the guides.

To make the two tiles blend evenly, they must have the same number of anchor points, and the should have the same width. If necessary, rearrange your guides by choosing View > Lock Guides to unlock them (no checkmark should appear), and then adjust them using the direct-selection (◈) tool. Then choose View > Lock Guides to check the command and lock the guides again. You can also release the guides (choose View > Release Guides), edit them as artwork, and then turn them into guides again (choose View > Make Guides).

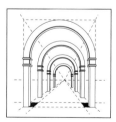

Before blending the tiles, you'll paint them.

4 Select the two tiles you just drew. Click the Fill box in the toolbox. Then select a color either by using the controls in the Color palette or by clicking a swatch in the Swatches palette.

5 With the two tiles still selected, click the blend tool (⬚) in the toolbox.

The blend tool creates a series of intermediate objects between the two selected anchor points. You can also blend between colors.

6 Click the corresponding point on each tile (for example, the upper left point on each tile.)

If you don't click the corresponding point on both tiles, the shapes won't blend evenly.

7 In the Blend dialog box, enter the number of tiles you want to create between the selected tiles. Note this number for the next part of the lesson.

The Blend dialog box displays a recommended number of steps, along with the percentage of change in the first and last steps, based on the two colors you are blending.

For example, if you blend two objects that are filled with 100% white and with 100% black, respectively, the program enters 254 in the Number of Steps text box because 254 is the maximum number of printable gray values between black and white on a high-resolution output device. (The total number of printable colors is 256—the starting color, the ending color, and 254 colors in between.) If one object is 50% black and the other is 100% white, the program enters 127 in the Number of Steps text box.

8 Leave the percentage of change at the default.

The default values are set by the value in the Number of Steps field. You can modify the percentage of change from the starting shape to the ending shape by entering any number between –100 and 200 in the First Blend and Last Blend text boxes.

For more information about blending, see "Blending shapes" in Chapter 7 of the *Adobe Illustrator User Guide* or in the online Help.

9 Click OK to blend the tiles.

10 If you're dissatisfied with the number of blended objects that results, choose Edit > Undo Blend Shapes. Then repeat steps 6 through 9, trying out other values.

Blending objects on top of objects

To complete the artwork, you'll make the foreground objects more detailed by adding layered shapes to the objects and using the blend tool again.

1 Draw triangles on the original left and right tiles, and fill them with white.

2 Select the two top triangles, and select the blend tool (⬚).

3 Click the corresponding points on both tiles.

4 For the number of steps in the Blend dialog box, enter the number of tiles you created in step 7 of the previous section. Click OK.

The blend tool lets you blend only between two selected objects at a time. You cannot blend between groups of objects. However, you can use the direct-selection tool to select the components of groups and blend between the components. You can also blend between two patterned objects if they are filled with the same pattern.

Now you'll complete the design on the tile.

5 Select the bottom left and right triangles. Repeat steps 3 and 4 to blend them.

Next, you'll group the tiles to apply changes to them as a unit.

6 When you've completed the design on the tiles for the foreground row, select all of the tiles and the triangles, and choose Object > Group to group them.

To complete the flooring, you'll use the scale tool again to create receding objects.

7 Select the group of tiles. Use the scale tool (⬚), and Option/Alt-click the vanishing point in the artwork.

8 In the Scale dialog box, enter a uniform scale percentage: use the same value that you chose in step 5 of "Making objects recede" on page 223. (We used 60%.) Select the Scale Line Weight option.

You can also choose to scale line weights automatically by selecting the Scale Line Weight option in the General Preferences dialog box. (Choose File > Preferences > General to display the dialog box.)

9 Click Copy to create additional receding tiles.

10 Press Command+D (Macintosh) or Ctrl+D (Windows) to Choose Arrange > Transform > Transform Again to repeat the scale and copy, and create as many additional rows of tile as you want.

11 Choose File > Close, save your changes if desired, and close the file.

This completes the perspective lesson.

Review

• How do you create guides?

You can draw or create artwork, or use existing artwork as a guide. You convert artwork into guides by selecting it and choosing View > Make Guides. You can then draw your artwork on top of the guides.

• How do you adjust the placement of guides?

You unlock the guides by choosing View > Lock Guides to uncheck the command; then you use the direct-selection tool to adjust the guides. Lock the guides by choosing View > Lock Guides again to check the command. You can also release the guides (choose View > Release Guides), edit them as artwork, and then turn them into guides again (choose View > Make Guides).

• Describe two ways to create perspective in your artwork.

You can simulate perspective using several techniques. (1) You can use the scale tool to scale and copy an object uniformly, and then repeat the scaling operation to make ever smaller (or larger) objects. (2) You can create a perspective grid that recedes toward a vanishing point, and then create your artwork using the grid as a guide. (3) You can use the blend tool to blend objects and make them appear to recede into the distance.

• How do you make objects blend evenly?

The two objects you blend must have the same number of anchor points, and you must click the corresponding point on each object for an even blend.

Lesson 17

Lesson 17

Drawing Cylinders

It's easy to transform two-dimensional circular designs into three-dimensional cylindrical shapes. You can also use gradients to give the illusion of depth. To create a true isometric drawing (drawn at 30°) use the values given in this lesson when scaling.

In this lesson, you'll learn how to do the following:

• Scale an object nonuniformly to simulate perspective

• Duplicate part of an object without grouping it with the original

• Move objects precisely

• Use the Transform palette to display an object's location

• Join objects

Creating an ellipse

You'll start the lesson by opening an artwork file. You can also draw an ellipse as the basis for your design.

1 Choose File > Open, and locate and open the Cylinder.ai file in the Lesson 17 folder. This folder is located in the Lessons folder in the AICIB folder on your hard drive.

(To see a sample of the finished artwork, open the Cylindr2.ai file in the Lesson17 folder, inside the Samples folder in the AICIB folder on your hard drive.)

2 Choose File > Save As, name the file Cylindr1.ai; then click Save.

3 Choose File > Close, save your changes if desired, and close the file.

You can also use the ellipse tool (○) to draw a circle or an oval, and then create the design for the top of the cylindrical object within the circle.

Next, you'll select the artwork and scale it precisely.

4 Choose Edit > Select All to select all of the artwork.

5 Select the scale tool (⬚) in the toolbox. Then Option-click the circle's center point.

6 In the Scale dialog box, select Nonuniform from the menu.

The Nonuniform option lets you enter values in both the Horizontal and Vertical text boxes.

7 Enter a value of 57.735% in the Horizontal text box, and 100% in the Vertical text box. Click OK.

(For a true isometric drawing, use a value of 57.735% for either the Horizontal or Vertical axis and then use 100% for the second value.)

8 Deselect the artwork.

Creating the cylinder bottom

Now you'll build the cylinder's bottom edge from a segment of the ellipse. You'll switch to Artwork view so that you can edit it more easily.

1 Choose View > Artwork.

To switch between Artwork and Preview view, you can also press Command+Y (Macintosh) or Ctrl+Y (Windows).

2 Use the direct-selection tool (⊢), and select the anchor point on the right side of the ellipse.

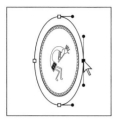

Next you'll copy and paste the arc.

3 Choose Edit > Copy to copy the arc.

4 Choose Edit > Paste in Front to paste the copied arc on top of the original ellipse. Do not deselect the arc.

Next, you'll move and copy the arc to create the bottom edge.

You can move the arc visually by dragging or precisely using the Move dialog box or the Transform palette.

5 If the Transform palette is not visible on-screen, choose Window > Show Transform to display it.

The Transform palette displays information about the location, size, and orientation of the selected object or objects. All values in the palette refer to the objects' bounding boxes (the transparent border that defines the boundaries of your artwork.)

6 Choose from these methods to move the arc:

• Use the selection tool to select the arc. Option-drag (Macintosh) or Alt-drag (Windows) the arc, holding down Shift to constrain the move. (Option/Alt-dragging creates a second copy of the arc.)

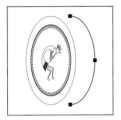

• Double-click the selection tool (➤) in the toolbox to display the Move dialog box (or choose Object > Transform > Move). In the Move dialog box, enter a value in the Horizontal text box for the depth you want the cylinder to be (we used 70 points); set the Vertical value to 0. A positive value moves the object to the right of the x axis. Click Copy.

```
┌──────────── Move ────────────┐
│ ┌─Position────────┐           │
│ │ Horizontal: 70 pt │  ┌─ OK ─┐  │
│ │                 │  └──────┘  │
│ │ Vertical: 0 pt  │  ┌Cancel┐  │
│ │                 │  └──────┘  │
│ │                 │  ┌ Copy ┐  │
│ │ Distance: 70 pt │  └──────┘  │
│ │ Angle: 0    °   │           │
│ └─────────────────┘           │
│ ┌─Options──────────────┐       │
│ │ ⊠ Objects ☐ Patterns │ ☐ Preview │
│ └──────────────────────┘       │
└──────────────────────────────┘
```

• In the Transform palette, position the pointer next to the existing value in the X (horizontal) text box, and type **+ 70 pt** to specify the amount of the move. Press Option+Return (Macintosh) or Alt +Enter (Windows) to copy the selection and apply the change.

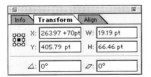

You can use this same technique of adding a value to an existing value (in other than the preset unit) in any Illustrator text box that accepts values. You can also subtract, multiply, divide, define percentages, and perform other mathematical operations in text boxes. For more information, see "Automatically converting units values in text boxes" in Chapter 3 of the *Adobe Illustrator User Guide* or in the online Help.

For more information about moving, see "Moving and Aligning Objects" (Chapter 6) in the *Adobe Illustrator User Guide* or in the online Help.

Attaching the cylinder bottom to its front

To complete the cylinder, you'll join the bottom edge to the front face of the cylinder.

1 Using the direct-selection tool (↘), Shift-click to select the top anchor points of both arcs.

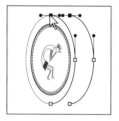

It's important to Shift-click with the selection tool and not drag. Dragging the selection marquee selects the ellipse underneath, in addition to the endpoints, and prevents you from joining the arcs.

2 Choose Object > Path > Join to draw a connecting segment between the two points.

(If you get an error message and cannot join the anchor points, you may have inadvertently grouped the copy of the arc with the ellipse at the beginning of the lesson, or you may have selected a point on the circle underneath the arc.)

3 Repeat steps 1 and 2 to select and join the bottom anchor points to complete the side of the cylinder.

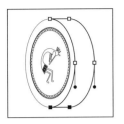

4 Press Command+Y (Macintosh) or Ctrl+Y (Windows) to return to Preview view.

Notice that the gradient fill from the circle was applied automatically to the side.

5 If desired, paint the side with another color or gradient. You can choose from various predefined gradients in Illustrator. We used a linear gradient.

6 If you paint with a gradient, use the gradient tool (▨) and drag in the artwork to adjust the gradient for a more realistic effect.

Experiment with dragging or clicking with the gradient tool until you get the results you want.

7 Choose File > Close, save your changes if desired, and close the file.

For more information about creating gradients, see Lesson 19, "Creating and Editing a Gradient Fill." For more information about painting, see Lesson 4, "Painting."

Review

• How do you scale precisely?

You Option-click (Macintosh) or Alt-click (Windows) to set the point of origin for the scaling and to display the Scale dialog box. Then you enter a value for the scaling in the dialog box.

• Describe two ways to move and copy a selected object simultaneously.

You can move and copy a selection several ways. (1) You can use the selection tool and Option-drag (Macintosh) or Alt-drag (Windows) an object. (2) You can use the Move dialog box to enter a precise value and then use the Move dialog box's Copy option. (3) You can use the Transform palette to enter a value for the move and then simultaneously copy and move the object by pressing Option+Return (Macintosh) or Alt+Enter (Windows).

Lesson 18

Lesson 18

Constructing Isometric Boxes

An isometric drawing positions the surfaces of an object at 30° to the viewer. To create an isometric view of a two-dimensional box, create a flat view, and then scale, rotate, and shear each panel of the box using a common point of origin. For a true isometric box, use the values given in this lesson.

In this lesson, you'll learn how to do the following:

• Start a flat view of a box

• Identify the point of origin used for all transformations in an isometric drawing

• Use precise values to create an isometric drawing

• Adjust line endings where lines meet

Starting with a flat view

The first step in creating an isometric drawing is to start with a flat view of the object. You'll use this flat view of the object (its top surface) to create the sides.

1 Choose File > New to create a new document.

If you want to work with existing artwork, skip to "Aligning objects around a common point" on page 245.

(To see a sample of the finished artwork, open the Isometr.ai file in the Lesson18 folder, inside the Samples folder in the AICIB folder on your hard drive.)

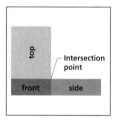

2 In a new or existing document, use the rectangle tool (☐) to draw the top surface as if it were standing on a side.

For precision, click rather than drag with the rectangle tool, and enter the panel's dimensions in the Rectangle dialog box.

Next, you'll create a side panel that fits precisely with the top.

3 Select the top panel. Select the rotate tool (○), and Option-click (Macintosh) or Alt-click (Windows) the lower right corner of the rectangle.

Option/Alt-clicking with a transformation tool lets you set the point or origin for the rotation, and displays the tool's transformation dialog box. Normally, Adobe Illustrator rotates a selected object from its center point.

4 Enter −90° in the Rotate dialog box, and click Copy to rotate and copy the original rectangle.

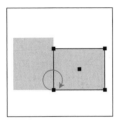

5 Using the selection tool (↖), drag the copied rectangle by its upper left anchor point until the cursor snaps to the lower right anchor point of the original rectangle.

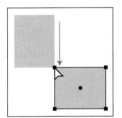

By default, the anchor points of objects snap to each other when they are within 2 points of each other. This behavior is useful for aligning objects, and is controlled by the Snap to Point option in the General Preferences dialog box. (To open the dialog box, choose File > Preferences > General.)

6 Deselect the artwork.

Next, you'll adjust the width of the side panel.

7 Using the direct- selection tool (⬚), select just the lower segment of the side panel. Begin dragging, and then hold down Shift as you finish adjusting the segment to the desired depth.

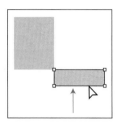

The Shift key constrains the adjustment horizontally or vertically.

Now you'll use the side rectangle as a model for the front panel.

8 Using the selection tool (▶), select the side rectangle.

When the direct-selection tool is selected, you can also click inside a filled object to select it (rather than using the selection tool).

9 Select the reflect tool (⬚); then Option-click (Macintosh) or Alt-click (Windows) the bottom left anchor point of the side rectangle.

Option/Alt-clicking lets you set the point of origin for the reflection. Normally, Illustrator reflects objects from the object's center point.

10 In the Reflect dialog box, select Vertical, enter a value of 90°, and click Copy to reflect a copy of the side panel.

When reflecting, positive values reflect counterclockwise; negative values reflect clockwise.

11 Deselect the artwork.

Next, you'll shorten the panel to the desired length.

12 Use the direct-selection tool (⟨⟩), and Shift-drag to align the left edge of the side panel with the left edge of the top panel.

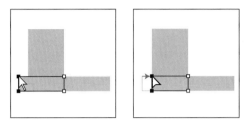

Adding design elements to the panels

Now that you've created a flat view of an object, you can add design elements to each panel before creating the isometric view. For example, you can paint the artwork, or add type, patterns, or other artwork to the box.

So that you can edit each panel as a unit, you should group each panel's design elements.

1 Select a panel and its elements.

2 Choose Object > Group.

3 Repeat steps 1 and 2 for each remaining panel.

Aligning objects around a common point

You will use the point common to all three panels as the point of origin to scale the rectangles and then shear and rotate each panel in the next steps. You'll start by opening existing artwork.

1 Choose File > Open, and locate and open the Isometr.ai file in the Lesson 18 folder. This folder is located in the Lessons folder in the AICIB folder on your hard drive.

If desired, you can work with your own artwork.

2 Choose File > Save As, name the file Isometr1.ai; then click Save.

A. Point of origin

3 Shift-click with the selection tool or choose Edit > Select All to select all of the panel artwork.

4 Select the scale tool (⌲), position the pointer on the point of origin where the three rectangles meet, and Option-click (Macintosh) or Alt-click (Windows).

5 In the Scale dialog box, choose Nonuniform from the menu.

6 Enter 100% in the Horizontal text box and 86.602% in the Vertical text box. Click OK.

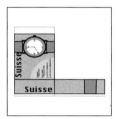

Use these exact values for a true isometric drawing. The nonuniform value foreshortens the flat view along the vertical axis so that subsequent shearing and rotation produce an isometric effect.

Now you'll shear and rotate the top panel to the right.

7 Select just the top panel of the package.

8 Select the shear tool (⌖), and Option-click (Macintosh) or Alt-click (Windows) the point of origin (the panel's lower right corner and the same point used in step 2). Enter 30° in the Shear Angle text box, and select the Horizontal Axis option. Click OK.

Keep the top panel selected.

9 Select the rotate tool and Option-click (Macintosh) or Alt-click (Windows) the point of origin. Enter –30° in the Rotate dialog box, and click OK.

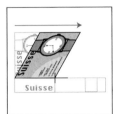 

Top sheared 30°
horizontally

Top rotated –30°
clockwise

You'll repeat the series of shearing and rotation to the front panel. In this case, you'll shear the panel by a negative amount so that the front panel is transformed in a clockwise direction.

10 Select the front panel.

11 Select the shear tool (⬚), and Option/Alt-click the point of origin. Enter –30° in the Shear Angle text box, select the Horizontal Axis option, and click OK.

Now you'll rotate the front panel into position.

12 With the front panel still selected, select the rotate tool and Option/Alt-click the point of origin. Enter –30° in the Rotate dialog box, and click OK.

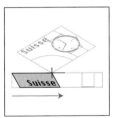 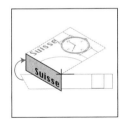

Front sheared –30°
horizontally

Front rotated –30°
counterclockwise

Again, you'll repeat the series of steps to shear and rotate the right side panel. In this case, you'll use positive values to shear and then rotate the panel in a counterclockwise direction.

13 Select the side panel.

14 Select the shear tool (⬚⤢), and Option/Alt-click the point of origin. Enter 30° in the Shear Angle text box, select the Horizontal Axis option, and click OK.

15 With the side panel still selected, select the rotate tool and Option/Alt-click the point of origin. Enter 30° in the Rotate dialog box, and click OK.

All the panels now fit together precisely to form the box.

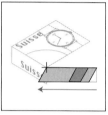 

Side sheared 30°   *Side rotated 30°*
horizontally   *counterclockwise*

Adjusting the line endings

As a final step if the artwork is stroked, you'll adjust the corner joins of the lines.

1 Using the zoom tool (🔍), zoom in very closely on the corner joins.

2 Check whether any of the corners extend past the intersection point.

3 Choose Window > Show Stroke. From the Stroke palette menu, choose Show Options to display all of the palette.

4 Use the direct-selection tool (▷) to select the protruding panel edges.

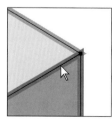

5 In the Stroke palette, click the Round Join button (the middle Join option).

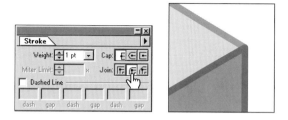

6 Double-click the zoom tool to zoom out again and fit the artwork in the window.

You can enhance the package's three-dimensional effect by painting each panel with a different tint of a spot color, or by adjusting each panel's color saturation.

For example, lighten the tint color of the top panel and progressively darken the tint on the front and side panels. You can also apply a gradient to one or more of the panels to give the impression of depth.

7 Choose File > Close, save your changes if desired, and close the file.

For more information, see Lesson 4, "Painting," or Lesson 19, "Creating and Editing a Gradient Fill," or see the related online Help topics.

For more information on the transformation tools, see "Modifying Shapes and Applying Special Effects" (Chapter 7) in the *Adobe Illustrator User Guide* or in the online Help.

Review

• Why is the point of origin significant when creating an isometric drawing?

The point of origin is the position from which a transformation starts. In the case of an isometric package, where the three panels of a box meet is the point of origin for all transformations.

• How do you set the point of origin using a transformation tool?

You select the transformation tool and Option-click (Macintosh) or Alt-click (Windows) where you want to set the point of origin. Option/Alt-clicking displays the tool's dialog box, and lets you enter precise values for the transformation.

• What values do you use to create an isometric drawing?

You scale the flat view of the artwork 100% horizontally and 86.602% vertically. Then you shear and rotate each panel by 30°.

Lesson 19

Lesson 19

Creating and Editing a Gradient Fill

A gradient fill is a graduated blend between two or more colors. You can easily create your own gradients. Or you can use the gradients provided with Adobe Illustrator and edit them for the desired effect.

In this lesson, you'll learn how to do the following:

• Create a new gradient

• Adjust a gradient in an object and across several objects

• Add colors to a gradient, including spot colors, and change their position in a gradient

• Change a gradient from a radial to a linear blend of colors

Creating a new gradient fill

Gradients can be used very much like colors to fill objects that you create. A *gradient fill* is a graduated blend between two or more colors or tints of the same color.

You'll begin this lesson by creating a new gradient fill.

1 Choose File > New to open a new file.

2 Select a drawing tool in the toolbox, and drag in the artwork to draw an object to fill with a gradient. Do not deselect.

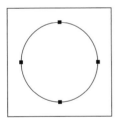

3 In the toolbox, click the Gradient button.

The Gradient button is beneath the Fill and Stroke boxes in the toolbox, and between the Solid Color and None buttons.

A default, black-and-white gradient appears in the Fill box in the toolbox.

Now you'll display the Gradient and Color palettes so that you can select another color for the gradient.

The Color, Gradient, and Stroke and Swatches palettes appear by default on the right of your screen. You use the Gradient palette to create your own gradients and —in combination with the Color palette and Swatches palette—to modify existing gradients.

4 If the Color palette is not visible on-screen, choose Window > Show Color.

The Gradient palette is grouped with the Stroke palette and appears when you display the Color palette unless you previously hid the Gradient palette.

5 If the Gradient palette does not appear on-screen, choose Window > Show Gradient.

6 Close the Info palette group. You won't need the palette for this lesson.

7 Click the Gradient palette tab to select the palette. Then position the pointer on the black arrow in the upper right of the Gradient palette, and drag to select Show Options from the palette menu.

8 Drag the Gradient palette from its group so that the Color, Swatches, and Gradient palettes are all visible on-screen.

9 In the Gradient palette, position the pointer on one of the color stops beneath the gradient slider, and drag to change the position of white and black. (The tip of the selected stop appears black.)

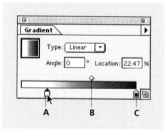

*A. Starting color stop **B.** Colors midpoint **C.** Ending color stop*

Notice how the gradient changes in your selected artwork.

In the Gradient palette, the left color stop under the gradient slider marks the gradient's starting color; the right color stop marks the ending color. A *stop* is the point at which a gradient changes from one color to the next. The diamond above the bar marks the colors' midpoint—where they blend equally.

In the Color palette, a color stop appears beneath the Fill box, indicating which color in the gradient is currently selected.

10 Now position the pointer in the color bar at the bottom of the Color palette, and in the color bar drag or click to select a new color.

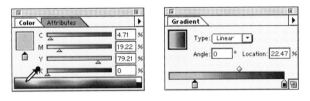

You can also drag the Color palette sliders, or you can Option-click (Macintosh) or Alt-click (Windows) a swatch in the Swatches palette to select a color. The selected color stop changes to reflect your choice.

Every gradient in Adobe Illustrator has at least two color stops. By editing the color mix of each stop and by adding color stops in the Gradient palette, you can create your own custom gradients.

11 Select the other color stop, and change its color by repeating step 10.

12 Save the gradient in the Swatches palette by dragging the swatch from the Gradient palette to the Swatches palette, or by clicking the New Swatch button at the bottom of the Swatches palette.

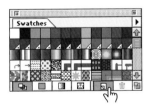

13 To display only gradient swatches in the Swatches palette, click the Gradient button at the bottom of the Swatches palette.

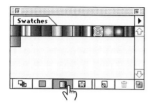

14 Try out some of the different gradients in your artwork.

You'll notice that some of the gradients have several colors. You'll learn how to make a gradient with multiple colors later in this lesson.

Adjusting a gradient fill

Once you have painted with a gradient, you can adjust its direction. Now you'll adjust a gradient in existing artwork.

1 Choose File > Open, and locate and open the Gradient.ai file in the Lesson19 folder. This folder is located in the Lessons folder within the AICIB folder on your hard drive.

(To see a sample of the finished artwork, open the Gradien2.ai file in the Lesson19 folder, inside the Samples folder in the AICIB folder on your hard drive.)

2 Choose File > Save As, name the file Gradien1.ai; then click Save.

3 Click the selection tool (⬩) in the tool box, and then click the left ball in the illustration to select it.

The ball is filled with a radial gradient fill that gradually changes from a yellow highlight in the center to orange at the edges.

Now you'll adjust the direction of the gradient.

4 Select the gradient tool (▓▓).

The gradient tool only works on selected objects that are filled with a gradient.

5 Drag the gradient tool across the selected object to change the position and direction of the gradient's starting and ending colors.

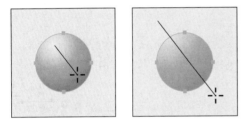

For example, drag within the ball to create a short gradient with distinct color blends; drag a longer distance outside the ball to create a longer gradient with more subtle color blends.

If you click inside the ball, you'll change the position of the highlight.

Editing a gradient

Now you'll edit the gradient and add some colors to it. First, you'll change the display of the Swatches palette so that you can choose any color from it.

1 If you want to see the effect of editing the gradient in your artwork, make sure that the ball is still selected.

2 In the Gradient palette, click the yellow color stop so that you can adjust its color. The Color palette displays the color of the currently selected stop in the Fill box.

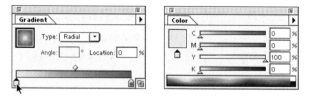

To edit the color of a gradient, you click a color stop below the gradient slider.

3 To adjust the midpoint, drag the diamond above the gradient slider to the right or left.

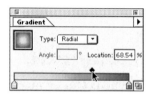

Notice the effect in your artwork.

4 Use one of these techniques to adjust the color:

• Option-click (Macintosh) or Alt-click (Windows) a color swatch in the Swatches palette to assign that color to the gradient stop. (To redisplay all of the swatches in the Swatches palette, click the Show All Swatches button [the leftmost button] at the bottom of the Swatches palette.)

• Use the sliders or enter a value in the Color palette to create a new color.

• Click or drag in the color bar at the bottom of the Color palette to create a new color.

• Select the eyedropper tool in the toolbox, and Shift-click a color in your artwork to copy it to the gradient stop.

Gradient colors can be assigned as CMYK process color, RGB process color, or a spot color. When a gradient is printed or separated, mixed-mode gradient colors are all converted to CMYK process color.

You can also add intermediate colors to a gradient to create a fill with multiple blends between colors.

5 In the Gradient palette, click anywhere beneath the gradient slider to add a stop.

You add a color to a gradient by adding a color stop. When you add a new color stop, a diamond appears above the gradient slider to mark the colors' new midpoint.

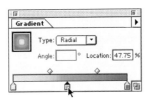

6 Follow step 4 to choose a color for the intermediate stop.

To delete a color, drag its color stop downward and out of the Gradient palette.

You can also edit a gradient by transposing colors or by changing the order of colors.

7 To transpose two colors in a gradient, Option-drag (Macintosh) or Alt-drag (Windows) any color stop to another color stop.

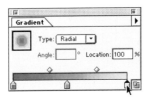

As you drag the icon, notice that the percentage value in the Location text box changes.

You can precisely distribute colors in a gradient.

8 To change the order of colors, select a color stop. In the Location text box, enter a new value from 0% (leftmost color) to 100% (rightmost color).

Yet another way to change the appearance of a gradient is to change the type of gradient.

9 In the Gradient palette, choose Linear from the Type menu to specify a linear change in colors.

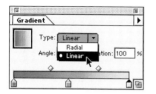

You can create a linear or radial gradient. With both types of gradients, you choose the starting and ending color of the fill. With a radial gradient, the starting point of the gradient defines the center point of the fill, which radiates outward to the ending point.

10 Now choose Radial from the Type menu in the Gradient palette.

The colors in the gradient now rotate outward from the starting color.

11 Click the New Swatch button at the bottom of the Swatches palette to save the gradient.

You can also edit a gradient by duplicating an existing one and then changing it.

12 Select a gradient swatch that you want to edit in the Swatches palette. Then click the New Swatch button at the bottom of the Swatches palette to duplicate a gradient swatch.

13 In the Gradient palette, edit the gradient as desired, following the steps in this section.

14 Save the edited swatch in the Swatches palette by clicking the New Swatch button at the bottom of the Swatches palette or choosing New Swatch from the Swatches palette menu.

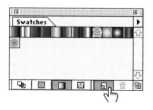

If you duplicate a swatch, you must save it in the Swatches palette to save any changes.

Using spot colors in gradients

You can use spot colors or tints of a spot color in the gradient.

1 Click the left color stop to change the starting color of the blend.

2 At the bottom of the Swatches palette, click the Show All Swatches button to display all of the swatches in the Swatches palette.

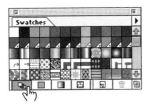

3 In the Swatches palette, Option-click (Macintosh) or Alt-click (Windows) a spot color to select it.

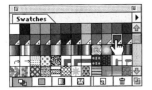

Spot colors are distinguished by a small white triangle when colors are displayed as swatches, and by a square with a dot in the center when colors are displayed by name. (You can change the display of spot colors by choosing Small Swatch, Large Swatch, or Name from the Swatches palette menu.) The Color palette also displays spot colors with their names.

Note: If you create a gradient between spot colors, you must deselect the Convert to Process option in the Separation Setup dialog box to print the gradient in individual spot color separations. For more information, see "Printing gradients as separations" in Chapter 16 of the Adobe Illustrator User Guide *or in online Help.*

Next, you'll create a gradient between two tints of the same color.

4 Click the right color stop to change the ending color of the blend.

To create a gradient between tints of a spot color, you select the same spot color for both the starting and ending gradient color, and then adjust the color's tint.

5 In the Swatches palette, Option-click (Macintosh) or Alt-click (Windows) the spot color you just selected in step 3.

To adjust the tint of a spot color, you use the Color palette. *Tint* is the strength (percentage) of a color.

6 In the Color palette, drag the T (tint) slider to adjust the ending color.

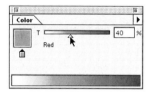

Now you'll fill the background with this new gradient.

7 Click the selection tool (▶), and click the background to select it.

8 Then click the Gradient button in the toolbox. The background is filled with the gradient you just created.

9 Deselect the artwork.

Changing a gradient throughout your artwork

You can change a gradient in your artwork across the entire document using the Gradient and Swatches palette. The gradient that you want to replace globally must first have been saved as a swatch in the Swatches palette.

1 Make sure that the gradient you want to replace throughout your artwork has been saved as a swatch in the Swatches palette.

If necessary, use the selection tool (▶), and select the gradient in your artwork. Select the Fill box in the toolbox or select the swatch in the Gradient palette, and drag it to the Swatches palette to save the gradient swatch.

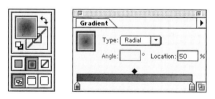

2 Command-click (Macintosh) or Ctrl-click (Windows) away from your artwork or choose Edit > Deselect All to deselect your artwork.

3 Use the Gradient palette to create a new gradient. (For help with this step, see "Editing a gradient" on page 258.)

4 Position the pointer on the Fill box in the toolbox, on the box in the Gradient palette, or on another gradient swatch in the Swatches palette.

5 Option-drag (Macintosh) or Alt-drag (Windows) the swatch over the gradient you want to replace in the Swatches palette.

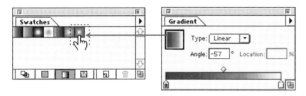

The gradient is replaced wherever it appears in your artwork.

To replace a spot color throughout your artwork, you use the same technique of selecting the replacement color, deselecting the artwork, and Option/Alt-clicking the swatch in the Swatches palette.

You can achieve some great effects with Illustrator's gradient tool, and you can also design your own gradations using the blend tool. Learn how in the "Gradations and blends" lesson in Module 5 of the online companion course, Mastering the Art. *See page 3.*

Adjusting a gradient in multiple objects

As a final step, you'll fill the type with a gradient and adjust its direction.

1 Using the selection tool, Shift-click to select all the letterforms in the poster titled "Milano."

(If you want to use your own type, first select the letterforms using the selection tool and choose Type > Create Outlines. The Create Outlines command converts the type to editable objects that can be painted with a gradient.)

2 In the Swatches palette, select a gradient.

Each object in the group is filled with the gradient. You must adjust the gradient to make it appear to blend across all of the letterforms.

3 Select the gradient tool (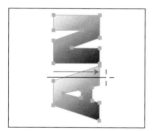), and drag across the objects from left to right to set the beginning and ending points of the gradient.

4 Deselect the artwork.

5 Choose File > Close, save your changes if desired, and close the file.

This completes the gradient lesson.

Review

• What is a gradient fill?

A *gradient fill* is a graduated blend between two or more colors or tints of the same color.

• Name two ways to fill a selected object with a gradient.

Select an object and do one of the following: (1) Click the Gradient button in the toolbox to fill an object with the default white-to-black gradient or with the last selected gradient. (2) Click a gradient swatch in the Swatches palette. (3) Make a new gradient by clicking a gradient swatch in the Swatches palette and mixing your own. (4) Use the eyedropper tool to sample a gradient from an object in your artwork and then paste it into the selected object.

• How do you adjust the blend between colors in a a gradient?

You drag one of the gradient's color stops in the Gradient palette.

• How do you add colors to a gradient?

In the Gradient palette, click beneath the gradient slider to add a color stop to the gradient. Then use the Color palette or color bar to mix a new color; or in the Swatches palette, Option-click (Macintosh) or Alt-click (Windows) a color swatch.

• What is a radial gradient? What is a linear gradient?

The colors in a radial gradient radiate outward from the starting color. The colors in a linear gradient change gradually along a linear path.

• How do you adjust the direction of a gradient?

You click or drag with the gradient tool to adjust the direction of a gradient. Dragging a long distance changes colors gradually; dragging a short distance makes the color change more abrupt.

• How do you replace or update a gradient throughout your artwork?

In the Swatches palette, you Option-drag (Macintosh) or Alt-drag (Windows) another gradient swatch over the gradient swatch you want to replace.

• Name two ways to edit a gradient.

You can add colors to a gradient. You can also change the type of gradient, from linear to radial. You can adjust the distance between colors in a gradient. You can also duplicate a gradient swatch in the Swatches palette, edit the gradient in the Gradient palette, and then save the edited gradient as a new swatch in the Swatches palette.

Lesson 20

Lesson 20
Path Patterns

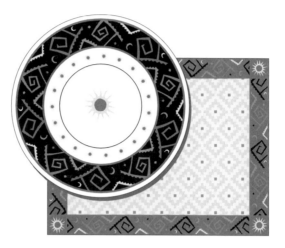

You can easily create border, outlining, and decorative effects by applying a path pattern to an object. You can modify any of the path patterns included in the Adobe Illustrator Path Patterns library. For example, change the color of a pattern, scale it, or add or delete elements to customize the pattern for your use.

In this lesson, you'll learn how to do the following:

• Paint with a pattern

• Distinguish between path patterns and fill patterns

• Customize and save patterns

• Transform a pattern that fills an object

Applying a path pattern

You can choose from libraries of patterns included in the Adobe Illustrator program, or you can create your own patterns from scratch using the drawing tools in Illustrator. The path patterns included in Illustrator have been optimized for stroking paths.

(Although you can use fill patterns and path patterns interchangeably to fill or stroke paths, interchanging types of patterns isn't recommended because the results may be unexpected.)

To begin the lesson, you'll open a document that contains several path patterns.

1 Choose File > Open, and locate and open the Pattern.ai file in the Lesson20 folder. This folder is located in the Lessons folder in the AICIB folder on your hard drive.

(To see a sample of the finished artwork, open the Pattern2.ai file in the Lesson20 folder, inside the Samples folder in the AICIB folder on your hard drive.)

This file contains the Aztec pattern, among other tribal patterns.

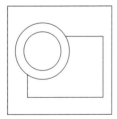

You can also draw a path that you'll use as a decorative border. Fill and stroke the path so that you can see it in Preview view—in most cases, any paint applied to the path will be covered by the path pattern.

2 Choose File > Save As, name the file Pattern1.ai; then click Save.

3 If you're not using the Pattern.ai file, open a path pattern document that you want to use.

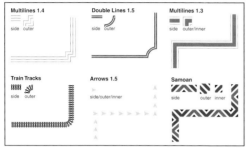

Path Pattern1 CMYK.ai file

A sample of path patterns is located in the Libraries > Path Patterns folder in Adobe Illustrator 7.0 application folder; an extensive series of path patterns is located in the Goodies folder on the Adobe Illustrator application CD-ROM.

To use any pattern, you must first open a file containing the pattern or its pattern tile.

4 Make the Pattern.ai file active.

5 Using the selection tool (➤), select the outer circle in the artwork.

6 Choose Filter > Stylize > Path Pattern.

7 In the Path Pattern dialog box, select the Sides box in the upper left corner to apply the pattern to the object's sides.

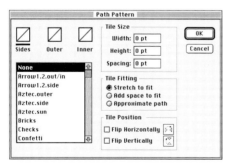

Path patterns can consist of up to three tiles—for the sides, outer corners, and inner corners of objects. The additional corner tiles enable path patterns to flow smoothly at corners. In contrast, fill patterns have only one tile.

8 From the scrolling list, click to select a pattern. (We used Aztec.side.)

The dialog box lists patterns from all open pattern files.

9 To get the effect shown here, use a Width value of about 150 points to scale the pattern tile up and double its width, and then press Tab.

Notice that the Height value changes to maintain a constant Width:Height ratio. Illustrator constrains the Width and Height values.

10 Make sure that the Stretch to Fit Tile Fitting option is selected so that the pattern is applied without gaps. Then click OK.

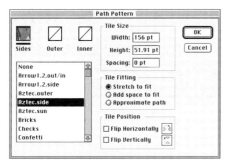

Spacing a path pattern

Next, you'll add spacing to a path pattern for a different effect.

1 Select the inner circle in the artwork. In the toolbox, click the Stroke box and change the stroke to None.

2 Choose Filter > Path Pattern.

Because the last filter you selected was the Path Pattern filter, the filter is now available from the Filter main menu and you do not have to select it from the Stylize submenu.

3 In the Path Pattern dialog box, make sure that the Sides box is still selected.

4 From the scrolling list, click to choose a pattern whose tile is an object on a background. (We used the Aztec.sun pattern.)

5 Click the Add Space to Fit option so that the objects will be spaced evenly around the inner circle.

6 In the Tile Size section, enter a Spacing value (we used 12 points). Then click OK.

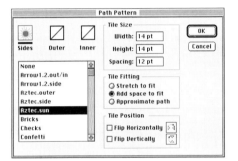

The pattern is applied to the path, and the path is deselected; the pattern elements remain selected. You can adjust the effect if you are dissatisfied with the results. Before making adjustments, you must delete any path patterns already applied unless you want to layer patterns along a path.

7 Choose Edit > Undo Path Pattern to delete the pattern that you just applied.

If you don't delete the pattern, subsequent path patterns you choose will be applied on top of previous patterns. In contrast, choosing a different fill pattern for an object replaces the original fill pattern with the new selection.

8 With the inner circle still selected, choose Filter > Path Pattern to display the Path Pattern dialog box.

You can use the keyboard shortcut—Option+Command+E (Macintosh) or Alt+Ctrl+E (Windows)—to display the dialog box for the last used filter.

9 Repeat step 6, entering a different Spacing value and clicking OK to adjust the space between the pattern elements.

Applying corners

Now you'll apply a path pattern to the rectangle, varying the corner tiles for the desired effect.

1 Select the rectangle, and in the toolbox, change its stroke to None.

2 Choose Filter > Path Pattern.

3 Make sure that the Sides box is still selected, and in the scrolling list select another pattern for the sides of the rectangle. (We chose Aztec.side again.)

You can distinguish path patterns and fill patterns in Illustrator by the suffixes that appear in the Path Pattern dialog box. Path patterns that come with Adobe Illustrator have suffixes that correspond to where the pattern should be applied to a path (its side, outer corner, or inner corner) or that are descriptive ("Aztec.sun"). Patterns supplied in Illustrator without suffixes are fill patterns.

Note the Height value for step 6.

4 Select the Stretch to Fit option.

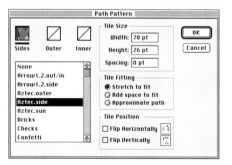

This option stretches each pattern tile as it's applied to prevent any gaps between tiles.

Now you'll choose a different tile for the outer corner of the rectangle.

5 Click the Outer box, and select a pattern that you want to use for the rectangle's corners. (We chose Aztec.outer.)

Path patterns tile perpendicular to the path (with the top of the pattern tile always facing outward). Corner tiles rotate 90° clockwise each time the path changes direction. In contrast, fill patterns tile by default like letters on a page, from left to right and downward (perpendicular to the *x* axis), but can be rotated and transformed.

6 If you chose a side pattern other than the example in step 3, adjust the Height value so that it matches the height of the side tile.

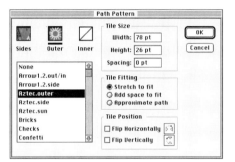

Corner tiles must have the same height as side tiles to align properly on the path. When you use a path pattern without a matching corner tile, you must adjust the height of the corner tile. (Corner tiles included in the Adobe Illustrator program have the same height as their corresponding side tiles.) If you plan to use corner tiles with your path pattern, align objects in the corner tile horizontally with objects in the side tiles, so that the patterns tile correctly.

7 If you are using your own artwork that has an irregularly shaped path, select the matching inner corner tile. Adjust the tile's height to match the side and outer corner tiles.

The inner corner tiles of path patterns included in the Adobe Illustrator program are reflected −135°, to match how the Illustrator program reflects corner tiles counterclockwise as it applies them to inner corners.

8 Select the Approximate Path option, and click OK.

The Approximate Path option offsets the pattern tile slightly from the path (rather than centering it on the path) to maintain the size of the pattern tile.

9 Choose File > Close, save your changes if desired, and close the file.

Customizing a path pattern

You can easily customize patterns included in the Adobe Illustrator program. The Adobe Illustrator application folder installed on your hard drive and the Adobe Illustrator Application CD-ROM contains several path pattern libraries.

You'll first open a document containing path patterns and their pattern tiles.

1 Choose File > Open, and open the Path Pattern2 CMYK.ai file or another path pattern file.

A sample of path patterns is located in the Libraries > Path Patterns folder in the Adobe Illustrator 7.0 application folder installed on your hard drive; an extensive series of path patterns is located in the Goodies folder on the Adobe Illustrator Application CD. The Libraries and Goodies folder also have fill patterns.

2 Using the selection tool (↖), select a pattern tile or pattern in one of the pattern files, such as the Aztec.outer pattern.

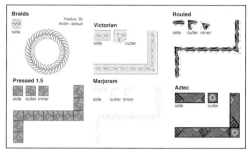

Path Pattern2 CMYK.ai file

Original Aztec.outer pattern

3 Choose Edit > Copy to copy the swatch or tile.

4 Make an existing artwork document active, or open a new document. Make sure that nothing is selected in the artwork.

5 Choose Edit > Paste to paste the pattern into the document.

6 Use the selection tool (↖) or the direct-selection tool (↘) to select artwork in the pattern tile.

The pattern tiles included in the Adobe Illustrator program typically are grouped with their pattern artwork. To select individual objects within a group, you must use the direct-selection tool.

7 Edit and paint the tile.

For example, change the color of individual elements in the pattern, or change the background color. You can also edit a pattern tile by deleting some of its elements or by adding new elements.

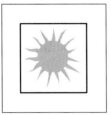

Customized Aztec.outer pattern

Defining a new pattern

Next, you'll define the pattern you just edited as a new pattern, and then save the pattern by adding it to the Swatches palette.

1 If the Swatches palette isn't visible on-screen, choose Window > Show Swatches.

2 If your artwork contains a bounding rectangle that you want to use to define the pattern, select the rectangle, and choose Object > Arrange > Send to Back. To make the rectangle invisible in the pattern, paint it with a fill and stroke of None.

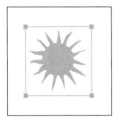

The Adobe Illustrator program builds a pattern from a pattern tile, which consists of the pattern objects (or artwork) surrounded by a rectangle (called a *bounding rectangle* or *bounding box*). Either you or the Illustrator program can create the bounding rectangle. If you draw a rectangle to define a pattern, the rectangle must be the backmost object in the artwork. If you do not draw a bounding rectangle around the selection, the Illustrator program uses an imaginary bounding rectangle that encompasses the selection.

3 Using the selection tool, drag the selection marquee to select all of the pattern artwork.

4 To make it easier to edit the pattern later, choose Object > Group to group the pattern elements.

5 To make the artwork a pattern, do one of the following:

• Choose Edit > Define Pattern. In the New Swatch dialog box, name the pattern. To organize your path patterns, name them with a suffix of ".side" for side patterns, ".outer" for outer corner patterns, and ".inner" for inner corner patterns. Then click OK.

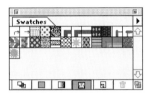

• Drag the artwork you want to use for a pattern onto the Swatches palette or onto the New Swatch icon at the bottom of the Swatches palette.

The new pattern is added automatically to the Swatches palette. Any patterns you add or import into a document are saved with the current document.

6 To paint with the pattern you just created, do one of the following:

• To stroke a path with the pattern, select the path and choose Filter > Stylize > Path Pattern. Choose where to apply the pattern—you can apply the pattern to the object's sides, outer corners, and inner corners. Adjust any other path pattern options, as you learned to do earlier in this lesson. Click OK.

• To fill an object with the pattern, select the object and click the Fill box in the toolbox; then click the swatch in the Swatches palette.

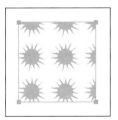

As you learned earlier in this lesson, the Path Pattern dialog box has various controls for adjusting the size of the pattern.

If you fill an object with a pattern, you can adjust the pattern's size, angle, or position within an object using the Transform commands. For example, you might want to scale or rotate the pattern.

7 Choose Object > Transform, and select the desired transformation from the submenu.

8 To transform just the pattern, in the dialog box that appears, select the Pattern option and turn off the Object option.

9 Enter a value for the transformation (a move, scaling, rotation, shearing, or reflection), and click OK.

10 Choose File > Close, save your changes if desired, and close the file.

For more information about creating path and fill patterns, see "Creating Gradients and Patterns" (Chapter 10) in the *Adobe Illustrator User Guide* or in online Help.

Review

• Describe two ways that path patterns differ from fill patterns in Adobe Illustrator.

Path patterns differ from fill patterns in a number of ways: (1) Path patterns are applied to the outline of an object; fill patterns paint the entire object. (2) You apply a path pattern to a selected object by choosing Filter > Stylize > Path Pattern; you apply a fill pattern by selecting a pattern swatch in the Swatches palette. (3) Path patterns can consist of up to three tiles—for the sides, outer corners, and inner corners of objects; fill patterns have only one tile. Illustrator applies path patterns perpendicular to the path; the program applies fill patterns perpendicular to the *x* axis. (4) Path patterns that come with Adobe Illustrator have suffixes that correspond to where the pattern should be applied to a path (its side, outer corner, or inner corner) or that are descriptive ("Aztec.sun"). Patterns supplied in Illustrator without suffixes are fill patterns. (5) Illustrator applies path patterns perpendicular to the path. By default, Illustrator applies fill patterns perpendicular to the x axis; however, you can rotate and otherwise transform fill patterns.

• Describe how to turn artwork into a pattern.

Select the artwork that you want to be a pattern and choose Edit > Define Pattern, or drag the pattern artwork onto the Swatches palette or onto the New Swatch icon at the bottom of the Swatches palette.

• How do you edit a pattern?

You edit a pattern by copying and pasting the pattern tile into your artwork, and then adding or deleting elements and changing any paint settings. Then you redefine the artwork as a new pattern by using the Define Pattern command or by saving the tile in the Swatches palette.

• What is a bounding box? How does it affect a pattern?

A *bounding box* is a rectangle that surrounds artwork. The Adobe Illustrator program builds a pattern by surrounding artwork (the pattern objects) by a rectangle; either you or Illustrator can draw this rectangle.

Lesson 21

Lesson 21

Printing Artwork and Producing Color Separations

The quality and color of your final printed output is determined by the process you follow to prepare an image for print. Whether you're printing a draft of your work on a desktop printer or outputting color separations to be printed on a commercial press, it's helpful to learn fundamental printing concepts to help you ensure that your printed results meet your expectations.

In this lesson, you'll learn about the following:

- Different types of printing requirements and printing devices
- Printing concepts and printing terminology
- Basic color principles
- How to separate your color artwork into its component colors for output to print
- How to use spot colors for two-color printing
- Special considerations when outputting to print

Printing: an overview

When you print a document from a computer, data is sent from the document to the printing device, either to be printed on paper or to be converted to a positive or negative image on film. For black-and-white, grayscale, or low quantities of color artwork, many people use desktop printers. However, if you require large quantities of printed output, such as a brochure or magazine ad, you'll need to prepare your artwork for output on a commercial printing press. Printing on a commercial press is an art that requires time and experience to perfect. In addition to close communication with a printing professional, learning basic printing concepts and terminology will help you produce printed results that meet your expectations.

Note: This lesson assumes that you have a desktop printer for use with the exercises. If you don't have a desktop printer available, read the sections and skip the step-by-step exercises.

Different printing requirements require different printing processes. To determine your printing requirements, consider the following: What effect do you want the printed piece to have on your audience? Will your artwork be printed in black an white? Color? Does it require special paper? How many printed copies do you need? If you're printing in color, is precise color matching necessary, or will approximate color matching suffice?

Let's take a minute to consider several types of printing jobs:

• A black-and-white interoffice newsletter, requiring a low quantity of printed copies. For this type of printing job, you can generally use a 300-to 600-dpi desktop laser printer to output the original, and then use a copy machine to reproduce the larger quantity.

• A business card using black and one other color. The term *two-color* printing typically refers to printing with black and one other color, although it may also refer to printing with two colors that are not black. Two-color printing is less expensive than four-color printing and lets you select exact color matches, called *spot* colors, which can be important for logos. For precise color matching, two-color printing is done on a printing press; if only an approximate color match is required, you might use a desktop color printer.

• A party invitation using two colors and tints of those colors. In addition to printing two solid colors, you can print tints of the colors to add depth to your printed artwork. Two-color printing is often done on colored paper that complements the ink colors, and may be done on a desktop color printer or on a printing press, depending on the desired quantity and the degree of color matching required.

• A newspaper. Newspapers are typically printed on a printing press because they are time-sensitive publications printed in large quantities. In addition, newspapers are generally printed on large rolls of newsprint, which are then trimmed and folded to the correct size.

• A fashion magazine or catalog requiring accurate color reproduction. *Four-color* printing refers to mixing the four process ink colors (cyan, magenta, yellow, and black) for printed output. When accurate color reproduction is required, printing is done on a printing press using CMYK inks. CMYK inks can reproduce a good amount of the visible color spectrum, with the exception of neon or metallic colors. You'll learn more about color models in the next section.

How do printing devices work?

Now that you've looked at several types of publications and different ways to reproduce them, you'll begin learning basic printing concepts and printing terminology.

Halftone screens

To reproduce any type of artwork, a printing device typically breaks down the artwork into a series of dots of various sizes called a *halftone screen*. Black dots are used to print black-and-white or grayscale artwork. For color artwork, a halftone screen is created for each ink color (cyan, magenta, yellow, and black); these then overlay one another at different angles to produce the full range of printed color. To see a good example of how individual halftone screens overlay each other at different angles on a printed page, try looking through a magnifying glass at a color comics page.

The size of the dots in a halftone screen determines how light or dark colors appear in print. The smaller the dot, the lighter the color appears; the larger the dot, the darker the color appears.

Screen frequency

Screen frequency (also called screen ruling or halftone frequency) refers to the number of rows or lines of dots used to render an image on film or paper. In addition, the rows of dots are broken down into individual squares, called *halftone cells*. Screen frequency is measured in lines per inch (lpi), and is a fixed value you can set for your printing device.

As a general rule, higher screen frequencies produce finer detail in printed output. This is because the higher the screen frequency, the smaller the halftone cells, and subsequently, the smaller the halftone dot in the cell.

However, a high screen frequency alone does not guarantee high-quality output. The screen frequency must be appropriate to the paper, the inks, and the printer or printing press used to output the artwork. Your printing professional will help you select the appropriate line screen value for your artwork and output device.

 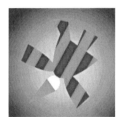

Low screen ruling (65 lpi) often used to print newsletters

High screen rulings (150-200 lpi) used for high quality books

Output device resolution

The *resolution* of a printing device describes the number of dots the printing device has available to *render*, or create, a halftone dot. The higher the output device resolution, the higher the quality of the printed output. For example, the printed quality of an image output at 2400 dots per inch (dpi) is higher than the printed quality of an image output at 300 dpi. Adobe Illustrator is resolution-independent, and will always print at the highest resolution the printing device is capable of.

The quality of printed output depends on the relationship between the resolution of the output device (dpi) and the screen frequency (lpi). As a general rule, high-resolution output devices use higher screen frequency values to produce the highest quality images. For example, an imagesetter with a resolution of 2400 dpi and a screen frequency of 177 lpi produces a higher quality image than a desktop printer with a resolution of 300-600 dpi and a screen frequency of 85 lpi.

About color

Before moving further into the printing process, let's stop for a few minutes and look at how color is produced, both by your computer monitor and by a printing device.

A color model is a method for displaying and measuring color. The human eye perceives color according to the wavelength of the light it receives. Light containing the full color spectrum is perceived as white; in the absence of light, the eye perceives black.

Color gamuts

The *gamut* of a color model is the range of colors that can be displayed or printed. The largest color gamut is that viewed in nature; all other color gamuts produce a subset of nature's color gamut. The following sections discuss two of the most common color models: red, green, and blue (RGB), the method by which monitors display color; and cyan, magenta, yellow, and black (CMYK), the method by which images are printed using four process ink colors.

The RGB color model

A large percentage of the visible spectrum of color can be represented by mixing three basic components of colored light in various proportions. These components are known as the *additive colors*: red, green, and blue (RGB). The RGB color model is called the additive color model because various percentages of each colored light are added to create color. All monitors display color using the RGB color model.

The CMYK color model

If 100% of red, green, or blue are subtracted from white light, cyan, magenta, or yellow is the resulting color. For example, if an object absorbs (subtracts) 100% red light and reflects green and blue, cyan is the perceived color. Cyan, magenta, and yellow are called the subtractive primaries, and form the basis for printed colors. In addition to cyan, magenta, and yellow, black ink is used to generate true black and to deepen the shadows in images. These four inks (CMYK) are often called *process* colors because they are the four standard inks used in the printing process.

Spot colors

Whereas process colors are reproduced using cyan, magenta, yellow, and black inks, spot colors are premixed inks used in place of, or in addition to CMYK colors. Spot colors can be selected from color-matching systems, such as the PANTONE or Toyo color libraries. Many spot colors can be converted to their process color equivalents when printed; however, some spot colors, such as metallic or iridescent colors, require their own plate on press. Use spot color in the following situations:

• To save money on 1-color and 2-color print jobs. (When your printing budget won't allow for 4-color printing, you can still print relatively inexpensively using one or two colors.)

• If you are printing logos or other graphic elements that require precise color matching

• If you want to print special inks, such as metallic, fluorescent, or pearlescent colors

Color management

Although all color gamuts overlap, they don't match exactly, which is why some colors on your monitor can't be reproduced in print. The colors that can't be reproduced in print are called *out-of-gamut* colors because they are outside the spectrum of printable colors.

To compensate for these differences and to ensure the closest match between on-screen colors and printed colors, Adobe Illustrator includes a Color Management System (CMS) that lets you select profiles for your monitor and for the output device to which you'll print. Selecting a color profile controls the conversion of RGB values to CMYK values at print time. To select a color profile, you use the Color Settings command.

1 Choose File > Color Settings.

2 In the Color Settings dialog box, select your monitor from the Monitor menu.

3 From the Printer menu, select the output device to which your artwork will be printed. (If you're printing a proof to a desktop printer first, select the desktop printer profile.)

Note: To determine the output device to which your artwork will be printed, talk with your printing professional. Once your job requirements have been assessed and an appropriate output device has been determined, you'll know which options to select in the Color Settings dialog box.

4 If you want the on-screen colors to simulate the printed output, select the Simulate Print Colors on Display option.

5 Click OK.

6 If you are printing a proof to a desktop printer and then printing to the final output device, be sure to select the profile of the final output device once you have printed your proof to a desktop printer.

Printing black-and-white proofs

As a general rule, you should print intermittent black-and-white proofs of all your documents to check the layout and to verify the accuracy of text and graphics before preparing the document for final output.

1 Choose File > Open. Locate and open the Circus1.ai file in the Lesson21 folder. This folder is located the Lessons folder within the AICIB folder on your hard drive. The four-color circus logo appears, which you'll print a draft of in black and white.

2 Choose File > Print; then click Print.

3 If you're not connected to a printer, go on to the next section.

The circus logo is printed in black, white, and shades of gray. Next, you'll work with printing color artwork.

Using the Document Info command

Before you take your color artwork to a prepress specialist or begin the process of creating color separations on your own, use the Document Info command to generate and save a list of information about all the elements of your artwork file. The Document Info command provides information about the objects, linked or placed files, colors, gradients, patterns, and fonts in your document.

If you're working with a prepress professional, be sure to provide the Document Info list to your prepress operator before delivering your files; they can help you determine what you'll need to include with your artwork. For example, if your artwork uses a font that the prepress house does not have, you'll need to bring a copy of the font along with your artwork.

1 Choose Edit > Deselect All. (If anything in the artwork is selected, the Document Info command becomes the Selection Info command.)

2 Choose File > Document Info. The Document Info palette appears.

3 Select different subjects about the document from the Info menu at the top of the Document Info dialog box. Each time you select a subject, information appears in the list box about the subject.

4 When you have looked through the information about the file, click Done to exit the dialog box.

Note: If you want to view or print the entire contents of the Document Info dialog box, you can save it and then open it in a text editor. To save the Document Info text, click Save, enter a name for the Document Info file, and then click Done. Open the file in any text editor to review and print the contents of the file.

Creating color separations

To print color artwork on a printing press, the composite art must first be separated into its component colors: cyan, magenta, yellow, and black, and any spot colors, if applicable. The process of breaking composite artwork into its component colors is called *color separation*.

1 Make sure the Circus1.ai artwork is still open. If you've closed the file, locate and open the Circus1.ai file in the Lesson21 folder. This folder is located the Lessons folder within the AICIB folder on your hard drive.

2 Click the selection tool in the toolbox; then select various objects in the artwork.

As you select different objects, notice that the Color palette reflects the current color's attributes. For example, if you click the flag atop the tent, a PANTONE color swatch appears in the Color palette; if you click the red part of the tent, the color is mixed using CMYK values.

Important: Each print job has specific requirements that you'll need to discuss with your printing professional before setting separation options in the Separation Setup dialog box.

3 Choose File > Separation Setup.

The Separation Setup dialog box includes options for specifying how the color in the artwork should be separated into its component colors, the output device and line screen to which the artwork will be printed, and whether the separation should be a positive or negative image. Before you see a preview of your artwork, you must select a printer description file to indicate which output device will be used to print your artwork.

Selecting a printer description file

PostScript Printer Description (PPD) files contain information about the output device, including its available page sizes, resolution, available line screen values, and the angles of the halftone screens.

1 In the Separation Setup dialog box, click Open PPD.

2 In the Lesson21 folder, locate and open the Printer Descriptions folder. Select the PPD that corresponds to the output device to which your artwork will be printed. (In this example, we selected the Linotronic 100 from the list of printer description files.) Click Open.

Note: A Printer Description folder with limited selections has been placed in the Lesson21 folder for this exercise. When you install Adobe Illustator, several PPDs are automatically installed, and additional PPDs are provided on the Adobe Illustrator CD.

The Options section of the Separation Setup dialog box is updated with the parameters for the Linotronic 100 imagesetter, and a preview of your artwork is displayed at the left side of the dialog box. (The preview of your artwork depends on the page size selected in the Page Size menu. Each output device has a variety of page sizes availble; select the desired page size from the Page Setup menu in the Separations Setup dialog box.)

In addition, printer marks surround the preview of your artwork. Printer marks help the printer align the color separations on press and check the color and density of the inks being used. The crop marks surrounding the artwork indicate where to trim the artwork after it's been printed.

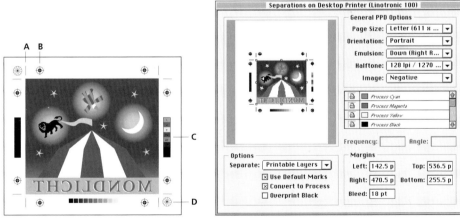

A: Crop mark B: Registration mark
C: Progressive color bar D: Star target

You can set your own crop marks to override the default crop marks in the Separation Setup dialog box. For information about how to set crop marks, see Chapter 13, "Producing Color Separations," in the Adobe Illustrator User Guide.

Separating colors

The circus artwork is composed of process colors and spot colors, which are displayed in the Separation Setup dialog box. By default, all spot colors are converted to their process color equivalents.

To the left of the process color names, a printer icon is displayed, indicating that a separation will be generated for each color. To the left of the spot color names, a process color icon is displayed, indicating that the spot colors will be converted to their process color equivalents. If you were to print color separations at this point, all the colors, including the spot colors in the artwork, would be separated onto the four process color (CMYK) plates, or pieces of film.

🖶	■	Process Cyan
🖶	■	Process Magenta
🖶	☐	Process Yellow
🖶	■	Process Black
☒	☐	PANTONE 116 CVC
☒	■	PANTONE 185 CVC

*Indicates spot color will be separated
into process color equivalents*

Composite image   Separations: Cyan   Magenta

Yellow   Black

As you learned earlier, you can print separations using process colors or spot colors, or you can use a combination of both. You'll convert the first spot color (PANTONE 116 CVC) to a process color, because a precise color match isn't necessary. The second spot color, PANTONE 185 CVC, will not be converted to a process color because a precise color match is desired. (In an actual situation, you'd output a spot color to its own plate only if a metallic ink or a specific logo color were required.)

To modify how individual spot colors are separated, you must first deselect the Convert to Process option in the Separation Setup dialog box.

1 In the Separation Setup dialog box, deselect the Convert to Process option.

Options		
Separate: Printable Layers ▼	🖨 ▪ Process Cyan	
☒ Use Default Marks	🖨 ▪ Process Magenta	
☐ Convert to Process	🖨 ☐ Process Yellow	
☐ Overprint Black	🖨 ■ Process Black	
	🖨 ☐ PANTONE 116 CVC	
	🖨 ▪ PANTONE 185 CVC	

A printer icon appears next to both spot color names, indicating that each of them will be output to a separate plate.

2 To convert the first spot color (PANTONE 116) to a process color, click the printer icon next to its name in the list of colors.

🖨 ▪ Process Cyan	
🖨 ▪ Process Magenta	
🖨 ☐ Process Yellow	
🖨 ■ Process Black	
☒ ☐ PANTONE 116 CVC	
🖨 ▪ PANTONE 185 CVC	

If you were to print at this point, five separations would be generated: one each for the cyan, magenta, yellow, and black plates (including the spot color converted to a process color); and a single plate for the PANTONE 185 CVC spot color. (This job would require a more specialized press, capable of printing five colors, or the paper would have to be sent back through the press to print the fifth color.)

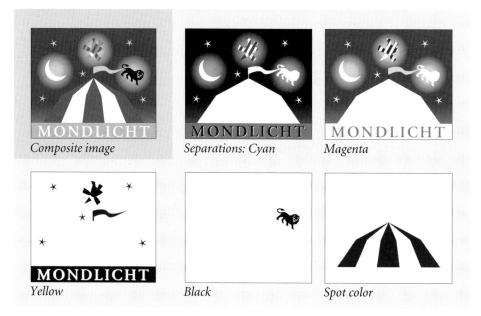

Composite image   Separations: Cyan   Magenta

Yellow   Black   Spot color

Specifying the screen frequency

At the beginning of this lesson, you learned the relationship between the output device resolution and the screen frequency determine the quality of the printed output. Depending on the output device you select, more than one screen frequency value may be available. Your printing professional will direct you to select the screen frequency appropriate to your artwork.

1 Choose 128/1270 from the Halftone menu in the PPD Options section of the Separation Setup dialog box. The first value, 128, represents the screen frequency (lpi), and the second value, 1270, represents the output device resolution (dpi).

Additional separation options, such as Emulsion Up/Down and Positive or Negative film, should be discussed with your printing professional. They can help you determine how these options should be set for your particular job.

2 Click OK to exit the Separation Setup dialog box.

Printing separations

Before printing your separations to a high-resolution output device, it's a good idea to print a set of separations, called *proofs*, on your black-and-white desktop printer. You'll save time and money by making any needed corrections to your files after reviewing the black-and-white proofs.

1 Choose File > Print.

2 From the Output menu, choose Separate.

3 In the Destination section of the Print dialog box, select Printer.

4 Click Print to print separations. Five pieces of paper should be printed—one for the spot color, and one each for cyan, magenta, yellow, and black.

5 Choose File > Save. The Separation Setup settings you entered are saved with your artwork file.

6 Close the Circus1.ai file.

Working with two-color illustrations

As you learned earlier, two-color printing generally refers to black and one other spot color, but may also refer to two spot colors. In addition to printing the two solid colors, you can print tints, or *screens*, of the colors. Two-color printing is much less expensive than four-color printing and allows you to create a rich range of depth and color when used effectively.

Editing a spot color

In this section, you'll open a two-color version of the circus illustration containing black, a spot color, and tints of the spot color. Before you separate the illustration, you'll replace the current spot color with another from the PANTONE color library. Illustrator lets you make global adjustments to spot colors and tints of spot colors using a keyboard shortcut.

1 Choose File > Open. Locate and open the Circus2.ai file in the Lesson21 folder. This folder is located the Lessons folder within the AICIB folder on your hard drive.

2 Make sure the Color palette and the Swatches palette are open and visible; if they aren't, use the Window menu to display them.

3 Click the selection tool in the toolbox; then click any colored part of the circus tent. Notice the PANTONE 116 CVC swatch in the Color palette.

4 At the bottom of the Swatches palette, click the New Swatch icon. Because PAN-TONE 116 is the current color in the Color palette, it is added to the Swatches palette as the new swatch.

Next, you'll replace every instance of the spot color (including any tints of the color) with another spot color.

5 Choose Edit > Deselect All before continuing.

6 Choose Window > Swatch Libraries > PANTONE Coated. The PANTONE color library palette appears.

You can choose new spot colors from the color library palette by typing the number of the color you want to use. First, you must use a key sequence to activate the palette's numeric entry capability.

7 To activate the palette for numeric entry, do one of the following:

• On the Macintosh, hold down Command-Option and click the mouse button on the PANTONE color library palette.

• In Windows, hold down Ctrl-Alt and click the mouse button on the PANTONE color library palette.

8 Now, type 193 on the keyboard. PANTONE 193 CVC is selected in the palette, and the fill swatch in the toolbox is updated to reflect the new color.

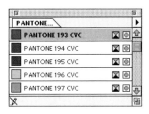

Next, you'll replace the current PANTONE color with the new PANTONE color.

9 Position the pointer on the fill swatch in the toolbox or the Color palette; then hold down Option (Macintosh) or Alt (Windows) and drag the pointer onto the PANTONE spot color you added to the Swatches palette (PANTONE 116 CVC). The artwork is updated with the new PANTONE color.

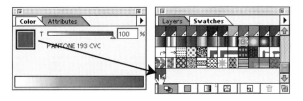

Separating spot colors

As you learned in "Separating colors" on page 298, you can convert spot colors to their process color equivalents, or you can output them to their own separation. When you're working with a two-color illustration, separating spot colors into their process color equivalents is less cost-effective than outputting the spot color to its own separation (four plates converted to CMYK versus one plate for each individual spot color). You'll deselect the Convert to Process option in the Separation Setup dialog box to output each spot color to its own separation.

Composite image   *Separation 1: Black*   *Separation 2: Spot color*

10 Choose File > Separation Setup.

11 Deselect the Convert to Process option. You'll notice that Process Black and the spot color PANTONE 193 CVC now have printer icons to the left of them in the list of colors for the artwork. The printer icon indicates that a single separation will be printed for each color. In addition, you'll notice the absence of icons next to cyan, magenta, and yellow in the list of separations, because the artwork contains no cyan, magenta, or yellow values.

12 Click OK to exit the Separation Setup dialog box.

13 Choose File > Save to save the Separation settings with your file.

14 Close the Circus2.ai file.

Creating trap

Trapping is used to compensate for any gaps or color shifts that may occur between adjoining or overlapping objects when printed. These gaps or color shifts are the effect of *misregistration*, which happens if the paper or the printing plates become misaligned during printing. Trapping is a technique developed by commercial printers to slightly overprint the colors along common edges.

Gap created by misregistration   *Gap removed by trapping*

Although trapping sounds simple enough, it requires a thorough knowledge of color and design, and an eye for determining where trapping is necessary. You can create trap in Adobe Illustrator using two methods: the Trap filter, for simple artwork whose parts can be selected and trapped individually; and by setting a Stroke value for individual objects you want to trap. Like printing, creating trap is an art that requires time and experience. For complete information about creating trap, see Chapter 16, "Producing Color Separations" in the *Adobe Illustrator User Guide*.

A simple kind of trap you can practice creating in this lesson is called Overprinting. You'll create a simple trap using this method.

Overprinting objects

When preparing an image for color separation, you can define how you want overlapping objects of different colors to print. By default, the top object in the Illustrator artwork *knocks out*, or removes the color of underlying artwork, on the other separations, and prints only the color of the top object.

You can also specify objects to *overprint*, or print on top of, any of the artwork under them. Overprinting is the simplest method you can use to prevent misregistration (gaps between colors) on press.

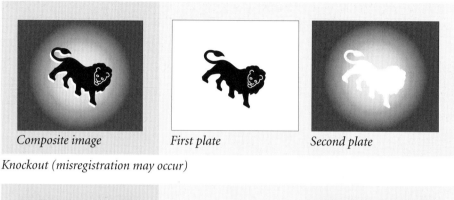

Composite image *First plate* *Second plate*

Knockout (misregistration may occur)

Composite image *First plate* *Second plate*

Overprint (black lion automatically traps into background color)

You'll select an object in the circus illustration and apply the overprint option. Overprinted colors cannot be previewed on-screen; they appear only when you print.

1 Choose File > Open. Locate and open the Circus1.ai file in the Lesson21 folder. The color version of the circus illustration appears.

2 Choose the selection tool from the toolbox and then click the lion to select it.

3 Make sure the Attributes palette is open. If the Attributes palette isn't open, choose Window > Show Attributes.

4 Click the Overprint Fill option in the Attributes palette.

If an object has a stroke, you can also select the Overprint Stroke option to make sure the stroke overprints on the object below it as well.

This concludes the Printing Artwork and Producing Color Separations lesson. Keep in mind that you must remain in close communication with your printing professional for each print job. Each print job has unique requirments you must consider before you begin the process of color separation.

Review

• How do the RGB and CMYK color gamuts affect the relationship between on-screen colors and printed colors?

Each color model has a gamut of color that overlaps, but does not precisely match the others. Because monitors display color using the broader RGB color gamut, and printed artwork uses the CMYK color gamut, there may be times when a printed color cannot precisely match an on-screen color.

• How can you create a closer match between your on-screen colors and printed colors?

You can select one of Illustrator's built-in color management profiles to better simulate the relationship between on-screen colors and printed colors.

• What is the benefit of printing interim drafts of your artwork to a black-and-white desktop printer?

It's a good idea to print black-and-white drafts of your artwork on a desktop printer to check the layout and the accuracy of text and graphics in your publication before incurring the expense of printing to a color printer or imagesetter (for separations).

• What does the term *color separation* mean?

Color separation refers to breaking down composite artwork into its component colors. For example, using the four process colors (cyan, magenta, yellow, and black) to reproduce the full spectrum of printed color.

• What are two ways to output spot colors?

You can convert a spot color to its process color equivalents if a precise color match is not required, or you can output a spot color to its own separation.

• What are the advantages of 1- or 2-color printing?

1- or 2-color printing is less expensive than four color printing, and you can use spot colors for precise color matching.

• What is trapping?

Trapping is a technique developed by commercial printers to slightly overprint the colors along common edges, and is used to compensate for any gaps or color shifts that may occur between adjoining or overlapping objects when printed.

• What is a simple method you can use to create trap?

You can specify objects to *overprint*, or print on top of, any of the artwork under them. Overprinting is the simplest method you can use to create trap, which prevents misregistration on press.

Lesson 22

Lesson 22

Preparing Images for Web Publication

The style of your artwork determines the file format you use to export the file for publication on the Web. For example, flat-color artwork should be exported to GIF89a format, and artwork containing gradients should be exported to JPEG format. When preparing images for distribution on the Web, your goal should be to create the smallest possible file while maintaining the integrity of the artwork.

This lesson shows you how to do the following:

• Determine which file format to use to publish different styles of artwork on the Web

• Export three styles of artwork for publication on the Web

• Link objects to URL addresses

Preparing images for the Web

The artwork in this lesson is a mock-up of a home page for distribution on the Web. The design of the completed page contains three styles of artwork —flat-color artwork, continuous tone artwork, and gradients.

1 Choose File > Open, and locate and open the Webpage.ai file in the Lesson22 folder. This folder is located the Lessons folder within the AICIB folder on your hard drive.

You'll begin this lesson by examining the completed Web page to see the various styles of artwork.

• Logo. The logo in the top right corner of the Web page is flat-color artwork.

• Buttons. The two buttons at the right side of the page are flat-color artwork with a transparency option applied, allowing the target-style background to show through the cut-out area of the buttons.

• Placed photograph. The photograph is a continuous-tone image imported from Adobe Photoshop.

• Gradients. The background surrounding the photograph contains a number of gradients in different shapes.

The following table describes the file formats generally recommended for outputting specific types of images for the Web. Keep in mind, however, that the file format you choose for your artwork may also be determined by the quality and size of the image you want to place on the Web.

Image	Export to
Flat color	GIF89a
Full color (continuous-tone)	JPEG or GIF, depending on quality desired
Gradient	JPEG
Grayscale	GIF89a
Black and white	GIF89a

Now you'll open individual files that contain the various parts of the completed Web page.

If you are creating Web graphics you may be using Adobe Photoshop and Illustrator together. Learn some advanced techniques to improve that powerful combination, including some tips on creating Web graphics, in Module 6 of the online companion course, Mastering the Art. *See page 3.*

Exporting flat-color artwork

Flat-color artwork should be exported to GIF89a format. Flat-color artwork appears best on the Web without any *dithering*—mixing colors to approximate those not present in the image.

You'll start by exporting the Web page flat-color logo to GIF89a format.

1 Choose File > Open. Locate and open the Logo.ai file in the Lesson22 folder.

2 To export the logo to GIF89a format, do one of the following:

• On the Macintosh, choose File > Export. Type logo.gif in the name text box; then choose GIF89a from the Format menu and click Save.

• For Windows, choose File > Export. Type logo.gif in the name text box; then choose GIF89a from the Save as Type menu and click Save.

The GIF89a Options dialog box appears. Using the Palette menu in the GIF89a dialog box, you select the color palette you want used to display the colors in the artwork.

Following is a brief description of all the palettes:

• The Exact option uses the same colors for the palette as those that appear in the artwork. No dithering option is available for the Exact palette, because all the colors in the image are present in the palette. The Exact option is available only if 256 or fewer colors are used in the artwork.

• The System (Macintosh or Windows) option builds a color table using the color table of the system you select. It is an 8-bit palette, capable of displaying 256 colors.

• The Web palette is a cross-platform 8-bit color palette. Use this palette option if your artwork will be displayed on various platforms or if you plan to display more than one illustration on the same page—for example, side-by-side illustrations—so that all the artwork is composed of the same colors on any platform.

• The Adaptive option builds a color table using the colors from your image. If you're displaying one image at a time (one illustration per page), choose the Adaptive palette option.

• The Custom palette lets you select a custom palette. To select a custom palette, click Load, and then locate and select a custom palette.

3 Choose Web from the Palette menu to use the standard Web palette to display the colors in your artwork.

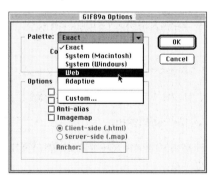

4 Select the Anti-alias option to smooth the edges of the logo.

5 Click OK to save the file. You can now open this file in any Web authoring application or any browser.

6 Close the Logo.ai file and do not save changes.

Linking objects to URLs

Any object you create in Adobe Illustrator can be linked to a Uniform Resource Locator (URL) string, transforming the object into a button that links a user to an Internet Web site. This feature is useful when designing image maps for Web pages, allowing you to preattach links to individual objects in an illustration before importing the artwork into a Web page design application.

To activate a URL link, you must export the artwork to GIF89a format and then open the artwork in a Web page design program or a Web browser.

You'll open a file containing the two buttons on the Web page, add URL links to the buttons, and then export the file to GIF89a format.

1 Choose File > Open. In the Lesson22 folder, select Buttons.ai from the list and click Open.

2 Click the selection tool in the toolbox; then drag a marquee around the top button (the guitar and the word "rock") to select it.

3 Choose Window > Show Attributes.

4 Enter the following URL in the URL text box: http://www.KCFM.com/rock.htm and press Return.

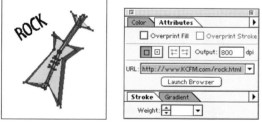

Select an object, and enter the corresponding URL address in the Attributes palette.

5 Now, select the second button and enter the following URL in the URL text box: http://www.KCFM.com/jazz.htm.

Note: The URLs in this lesson are fictitious; if you want to test a working URL, try using the http://www.adobe.com address for one of the buttons.

After assigning the URLs to the buttons, you can verify that the URL is valid by using the Launch Browser button in the Attributes palette if your computer has an Internet browser (such as Netscape Navigator or Microsoft Internet Explorer).

6 If your system is connected to an Internet browser, click the Launch Browser button to automatically open the browser and connect to the URL you defined as the object's link. If your system isn't connected to an Internet browser, go to the next step.

7 To export the buttons to GIF89a format, do one of the following:

• On the Macintosh, choose File > Export. Type Buttons.gif in the name text box; then choose GIF89a from the Format menu and click Save.

• For Windows, choose File > Export. Type Buttons.gif in the name text box; then choose GIF89a from the Save as Type menu and click Save.

8 Choose Web from the Palette menu.

Next, you'll select the Transparent option and apply it to the buttons. The Transparent option applies transparency to all the unpainted areas surrounding the artwork and also to any cutout areas within the artwork. For the Web page in this lesson, the Transparency option must be applied to the buttons to be able to see the target-shaped background behind them.

*Result of button displayed in browser without
transparency option and with transparency option*

*Note: In Illustrator, you cannot specify which areas you want to make transparent; the
transparent areas are defined based on the unpainted areas of the artwork.*

9 Select the Transparent option in the GIF89a dialog box.

10 Select the Anti-alias option to smooth the edges of the buttons.

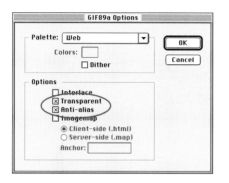

Next, you'll select the Imagemap option to include the link addresses with the exported GIF89a file.

11 Choose Imagemap from the Options section of the dialog box; then select the Client-side option.

The Client-side saves two files: the .gif file containing the artwork, and an .html file containing the link information. These two files must be saved in the same location to be interpreted by the Web page creation application.

12 Click OK to save the file. Two files are written: an html file containing the link information and a file containing the button artwork.

Note: The names of the two saved files are based on the name of the document. For example, for a document named Buttons, the art filename would be Buttons.gif, and the html file would be named Buttons.html.

13 Close the Buttons.ai file and do not save changes.

14 If you have a Web browser or a Web page creation application on your system, launch the program. (If you don't have an appropriate Web application, you can look at the illustrations in this book to see how the URL links work with the buttons.)

15 In the Web application, choose File > Open, and open the file with the .html extension.

16 Position the pointer over one of the buttons; the URL address appears (if you're using Netscape, the URL address appears in the lower left corner of the window).

*Use a browser or Web page design
application to verify the URL link.*

17 Follow the instructions in your Web creation application or Web browser to activate the link.

Note: *If the URL string does not appear when you position the pointer over the object, the .gif file and the .html file are not in the same location. Move the two files into the same location.*

Exporting continuous-tone and gradient artwork

Continuous-tone artwork and artwork containing gradients are generally saved to JPEG file format. JPEG saves files using different compression options. The compression option you choose for artwork determines how the color information in the image is preserved, which affects the size and quality of the artwork.

Note: Although JPEG is the recommended file format for continuous-tone artwork, you can save continuous-tone artwork to GIF89a format. There may be times when you want to apply a GIF option to continuous-tone artwork, such as linking the artwork to a URL. Keep in mind that saving continuous-tone artwork to GIF89a format may compromise the quality of the artwork.

You'll open and export the part of the Web page containing the photograph and the surrounding gradients.

You'll export the photograph and gradient background portion of the Web page to JPEG format using two different compression options. After you've exported the files, you'll open them and compare the differences in the size and quality of the artwork.

1 Choose File > Open. Locate and open the Lesson22 folder, select the Photo.ai file, and then click Open.

2 To export the artwork to JPEG format, do one of the following:

• On the Macintosh, choose File > Export. Type the name Jpeg1o.jpg, choose JPEG from the Format menu, and then click Save.

• For Windows, choose File > Export. Type the name Jpeglo.jpg; then choose JPEG from the Save as Type menu and click Save.

The JPEG dialog box appears, from which you select compression options.

3 In the JPEG Options dialog box, drag the slider to the left or enter 1 in the text box to select Low image quality compression. The lower the image quality, the higher the amount of compression applied, resulting in a smaller file.

4 Click OK.

The jpeglo.jpg file is created and is saved in the Lesson22 folder.

5 Follow the instructions in step 2 to export another copy of the file, but this time, name the file jpeghi.jpg. Once you've completed step 2, go on to step 6.

6 In the JPEG Options dialog box, drag the slider to the right or enter 10 in the text box to select High image quality compression. The higher the image quality, the lower the amount of compression applied, resulting in a larger file.

7 Click OK to export and save the jpeghi.jpg file.

8 Choose File > Close to close the Photo.ai file before continuing.

Now, you'll open both JEPG files and compare the differences in the quality of the artwork.

9 Choose File > Open, select jpeglo.jpg from the list of files, and then click Open.

10 Choose File > Open, select jpeghi.jpg from the list of files, and then click Open.

11 Make sure that both photos are displayed at a 100% view, and then align the photos side-by-side.

You'll notice a difference in image quality between the two files, particularly around the arrow, the note, and where gradient elements join edges. In this example, the file size of the jpeghi.jpg file is approximately 192K, and the jpeglo.jpg file is approximately 64K. If image quality is not of primary importance, the 64K file will download much more quickly than the 192K file.

12 Close all the open files and do not save changes.

Review

• What determines the file format you should use when saving images for Web publication?

The type of image you're working with determines the file format you should use to save an image for publication on the Web. In addition, file size and image integrity may be used to determine which file format you use. In general, you should attempt to maintain the integrity of the image and keep the file size down.

• What is the benefit of selecting the Web palette when preparing images for publication on the World Wide Web?

Selecting the Web palette ensures that your images are displayed using the same color palette, regardless of the platform on which the image is displayed.

• What does anti-aliasing do?

Anti-aliasing smooths the edges of objects.

• What does transparency do?

In Illustrator, transparency makes all the unpainted areas of the artwork transparent in a Web browser. You cannot select specific areas to be transparent; only the unpainted areas are defined as transparent.

Index